COME WITH ME
TO
INDIA

On A Wondrous Voyage Through Time

COME WITH ME TO INDIA

On A Wondrous Voyage Through Time

By

Sudha Koul

🌿 Cashmir, Inc. 🌿 Pennington, New Jersey

Koul, Sudha
Come With Me To India
On A Wondrous Voyage Through Time

Copyright ©1997

Library of Congress Catalog Card Number 96-092966

ISBN 0-9624838-2-6

Address Inquiries To:

Cashmir, Inc.
P.O. Box 111
Pennington, New Jersey 08534
1-800-609-8266

For
Keya & Yashomati

Contents

Foreword

I was born in India, but came to the United States of America right after I was married in 1974. My husband and I have made America our new home, and this is where we have brought up our two daughters. One has just graduated from college, and the other is a junior in high school. As very American children with Indian parents, our daughters have enjoyed the special privilege of being a part of two cultures, two heritages. However, I realize that since they have lived in the United States all their lives, except for holiday visits to their grandparents and other relatives in India, they have not truly had the time to understand their ancestral land and its history. This book has been written with this realization in mind. I want to share what I know about India with them, the events or facts *I* find so fascinating about Indian history, lifestyles, travel, science, in short, anything, and everything. In fact, researching and writing *Come with me to India* was a journey of discovery and rediscovery for me as well. If at some time my daughters' curiosity about India is similarly satisfied by this book, my purpose will have been served. On a more universal note, I hope that others who might have questions about India, will also find the book useful.

Although *Come with me to India* is presented in the year which celebrates India's fiftieth anniversary of independence, it has many years of thought and preparation behind it. In the past sixteen-odd years I have often been asked by the teachers in my daughters' schools to speak about India, either because the students were "doing India" in Social Studies or because the teachers desired to bring some cultural diversity to the class. My speaking career at this very personal level was an enjoyable task that I felt honored to perform. There were many questions from the children as well as from the teachers, and on every such visit, I noted the "most-often-asked" or "most intriguing" questions.

I would come away from these classroom visits fully intent upon formally collecting my notes and putting them together in a book, but I never quite got down to the job. Then last year, a school librarian remarked on the paucity of school books containing basic information about India. Several teachers concurred. If anything, these comments provided the green light in my mind for this book that had been half-written for years in my notes and in my heart. I hope that *Come with me to India* proves to be as helpful as it is intended to be. I certainly do not expect it to satisfy everyone, but if it provokes further reading or a search for more detailed information, I will consider myself more than adequately recompensed.

I could not have brought this book to completion by myself. I thank first of all my husband and my daughters, who have always been an inspiration and a great support to me and with whom I feel blessed to share an Indian home in a New Jersey suburb. I also thank the schoolteachers who were eager to bring India to their classrooms and the children with *so many* wonderful questions.

I would like to thank some others as well. My heartfelt gratitude goes to Dr. Atul Kohli, Professor of Political Science at Princeton University, for allowing me to impose upon him and for agreeing to take a look at the manuscript. His encouragement and response have been absolutely vital to me. Dr. Aaditya Mattoo, economist at the World Trade Organization in Geneva, Switzerland, was kind enough to comment on the chapter on the Indian economy. I deeply appreciate his sharing some of his invaluable time with me. My gratitude goes to Dr. Yoel Arbeitman and Dr. Ephraim Isaac, scholars, linguists, and erstwhile colleagues at the Institute of Semitic Studies, Princeton, New Jersey, for their illuminating discourse. Dr. Suvir Kaul, Professor of English at Stanford University, California, generously found time to comment on the text, and I am grateful to him as well.

I would also like to thank Rayman Mathoda, freshly graduated with a B.A. from Princeton University, for finding the time, at a busy juncture in her own professional life, to assist me in my research. Her help was indispensable. Betty Burns has once again as my editor cleaned up my act and made some sense of the manuscript. Betty teaches at The Pennington School in Pennington, New Jersey. I am deeply indebted to her for finding time for this book in spite of a hectic schedule. Keya Koul, my perspicacious editorial assistant, came to the rescue as the book neared completion and helped finalize the manuscript. I am extremely thankful to her. Any shortcomings the reader might find in *Come with me to India* are entirely my responsibility.

Finally, I owe this book to a great teacher, my grandfather and friend, Prof. S.L. Dhar.

Sudha Koul
Pennington, 1997

Note

India achieved independence from Great Britain on August 15, 1947. Prior to that date India, the "jewel" in the British Crown, meant the *entire* Indian subcontinent. At independence, the subcontinent was partitioned into two sovereign nations, India and Pakistan. A part of Pakistan, known as East Pakistan (East Bengal), was situated in eastern India. In 1971 East Pakistan achieved independence from Pakistan and became a sovereign nation called Bangladesh. For the purposes of this book, references to events in India before August 15, 1947, pertain to the entire Indian subcontinent, and references to events in India after that date pertain to the Sovereign Democratic Republic of India.

The capital of India is New Delhi; the capital of Pakistan is Islamabad; and the capital of Bangladesh is Dhaka.

Part One

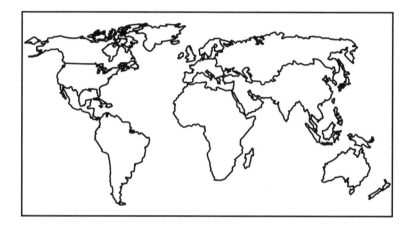

CHAPTER ONE

Why are we going to India?

Are your parents or grandparents from India? Are any of your classmates from India? Do you have neighbors from India? Have you been studying India in your classroom? Have you wondered what Indians have in common with Native Americans, who used to be called Indians? Do you have an Indian restaurant in your shopping center? Have you wondered why some Indians speak very British-sounding English? Do you want to know why some Indians wear a mark or a "dot" on their foreheads? Do you wonder what the word *Raj* means? On your last stop at the rice section of your supermarket, did you wonder what *Basmati* is? Have you ever met anyone wearing a *sari* (a flowing Indian dress) or a turban and wondered, "Who are these people and what exotic language do they speak?" Do you want to know if tigers and elephants still roam in that ancient and mysterious land? Do you wonder what level of technology there is in India? Do you wonder how many people of Indian descent live in the United States?

If the answer to any or all of these questions is YES! then this book invites you to visit India and become acquainted with her. Come with me to India, the land where I was born, on this sturdy little *vahana* (vehicle or flying machine) made of paper and words.

CHAPTER TWO

How do we get to India?

India is several thousand miles away from either coast of the United States of America. Just to give you some idea of the distance, it takes about sixteen hours of flying time between New York and New Delhi. If you count the time it takes you to get to the airport and the stopover at another airport midway, it will take you almost a day and a night getting to India. You will then arrive at one of the country's four major international airports. The major international airports in India are New Delhi in the north, Bombay in the west, Madras in the south, and Calcutta in the east.

If you were to fly from New York to New Delhi in a straight line, you would fly east over the Atlantic Ocean, over Europe, over the Middle East, over Afghanistan, over Pakistan, and finally into India. If your airplane is due to land at Bombay, which is on the western coast of India, you would fly over the Arabian Sea for the last portion of your flight. Flying from the west coast of the United States to India in a straight line, you would fly over Japan, China, and Myanmar (Burma) and land at Calcutta in the east of India. Once you arrive at any of the international airports, you can take connecting flights into most other cities in India. There are many Indian national airlines, and there are about a hundred regularly-operating airports in India.

If you go by sea on any of the major shipping lines to India, you may arrive at Bombay or Goa on the west coast or at Madras or Calcutta on the east coast. These are some of the major ports for passenger ships, but there are many ports for freight, some of which have existed for centuries (as you will find out later).

After you arrive at a major Indian city or port, you can also make connections by train or bus to your next destination. There are roughly 40,000 miles of railroads in India. In fact, the Indian train network is so widespread that I often think India's railroad maps resemble the capillaries in the human circulatory system! Train tickets are priced according to the level of comfort desired so you can choose between hardwood-bench asceticism or the comfort of cushioned seats and air-conditioning. As for buses, they ply everywhere. Some are good; some are not so good. For sightseeing, the best idea would be to take tour buses supplied by a dependable travel agency.

So, you're finally at your destination city in India. Where will you stay? Don't worry. India has had tourists for over two thousand years so it is well-prepared to receive guests. If you are not staying at the home of a friend or a relative, you can stay at a hotel. Once again, you can stay in a five-star luxury hotel (India's luxury hotels are among the best in the world), or you can stay at a four-, three- or two-star hotel. It all depends on how much you want to pay. In either case, you will soon feel at home as have *many* others before you.

CHAPTER THREE

What terrain, flora, and fauna will we find?

India is a land of dramatic contrasts in geography. The Himalayas, which form the northern wall for India and her neighbors, Nepal and Pakistan, are home to some of the tallest peaks and ranges in the world. Among these peaks are Mount Everest in Nepal, K2 and Nanga Parbat in Pakistan, and Kanchenjunga (India's tallest peak) and Nanda Devi in India. The magnificent Himalayan ranges extend from the northwest to the northeast of India like protective arms; the ranges on India's northernmost frontier are the Ladakh Range, the Zanskar Range, and the Pir Panjal Range. Nestled between these ranges is the valley of Kashmir, my beloved and beautiful birthplace.

Moving southwards the Himalayan mountains then slope down into the flat part of India, leveling into the Indo-Gangetic Plains, commonly called the *plains*. The plains spread across the north down to central India. To the northwest of the plains lies the Thar desert in Rajasthan, the Indian State of fabled palaces and *Maharajas* (Princes). There are several mountain ranges all over the rest of India, but these are much lower than the Himalayas. Of these mountains, the Vindhya and Satpura range of mountains coming out of the west, halfway across India, seem to separate the northern plains from the south. These mountains flatten as they move towards the south, and the land then forms the Deccan plateau which covers most of south India. This plateau, which is just below central India, is a flat table with an eastward incline. We are now in the peninsular part of India.

South of the Vindhyas and the Satpuras, the peninsular land mass becomes triangular with the southernmost part of India narrowing down to a point called Kanya Kumari (Cape Comorin) which juts out into the Indian Ocean. The coastal sides of this peninsula are bordered by low mountain ranges called the Eastern and Western Ghats. Just off Kanya Kumari is the island country of Sri Lanka (formerly Ceylon).

With a little bit of imagination you can say that India is shaped like a diamond: narrow at the top, wide in the middle, and then narrowing to a point down at the bottom. As I always say, a gem of a country!

The waters flanking the peninsular coast of India are the Bay of Bengal on the east and the Arabian Sea on the west. The Bay of Bengal is home to the Andaman and Nicobar Islands, and the Arabian Sea is home to the Lakshadweep Islands. These islands are India's offshore territories. The peninsular subcontinent is surrounded by the Indian Ocean.

The tremendous range of geography in India (tropical and coastal in the south and alpine and desert in the north) makes for tremendous variety in flora, fauna, and my favorite subject, cuisine. I grew up surrounded by narcissi and apple orchards, and my friends in the south wore tropical flowers in their hair and used coconuts in the dishes they prepared.

Where is India located on the great continent of Asia? As I mentioned earlier, the southernmost tip of India lies just above the island of Sri Lanka, an independent sovereign state, which has great cultural ties to India. Traveling to the east, we find Bangladesh situated in the eastern seaboard of India; its three sides are surrounded by Indian states and the fourth side is on the Bay of Bengal. Further east we meet Myanmar (formerly Burma) and then to the northeast lie

Nepal and Bhutan. Beyond these surrounding countries are Tibet and China. The states of the former U.S.S.R. lie to the north of India, and to the northwest we find Pakistan and Afghanistan, leading to Iran, the Gulf states, Saudi Arabia, and the Middle East. These are important places to remember because all these countries have profoundly influenced the rich history of India.

What is the weather in India like? Most of India has three main seasons: a very mild winter; an extremely hot summer (some areas can reach temperatures of 115 degrees Fahrenheit); and the rainy season, also known as the monsoons. Although heat and monsoons are the predominant factors in the climate of most of India, the parts of the country which are near or in the Himalayan mountain areas experience colder winters and milder monsoon weather. In fact, seasons there are very similar to winter, spring, summer, and autumn as we know them here in the United States. There is also a great deal of snow in these areas, and on quite a few of the mountain tops the snow never melts. This makes for some rather breathtaking snowscapes and makes clear why the word "Himalaya" means the Abode of Snow.

The snows of the Himalayan glaciers give birth to some of the great rivers of India. Of these rivers the Indus in the north, the Ganges flowing across the north and northeast, and the Brahmaputra in the east, constitute the main river systems. In addition to the rivers born of Himalayan snows are those that originate from the mountains of central and south India. Going south of the Vindhya range these rivers are the Narbada, the Tapti, the Godavari, the Krishna, the Mahanadi, the Tungabhadra, and the Kauvery. There are many other smaller but equally cherished and eulogized rivers in India. It is easy to see why transportation by water is so time-honored and widespread in India.

The rivers of India are major factors in its economy and agriculture, but, interestingly, the main source of irrigation still is the water from the torrential summer rains of the monsoons. These waters cool the intense summer heat and give life to agriculture and thus to the people. Capricious as they are, the monsoons have always had the upper hand in the economy and life of India. They are the greatest assurance of continuity, prosperity, and happiness in the subcontinent and inspire some of the most lyrical and romantic Indian poems and songs. Unfortunately, there are often times when the rains provide too much of a good thing, and flooding from monsoons causes ravaging loss of life and property. To provide protection from these natural disasters and to tame and utilize the energy of the rivers, India has undertaken many engineering projects, such as the Bhakra Nangal Dam and the Damodar Valley Project.

One-fifth of the land surface in India is covered by the deciduous, evergreen, and semi-evergreen forests which are found in different areas of the country. The Himalayan foothills are covered by pine and deciduous forests, and in these parts one may see conifers, junipers, birches, maples, etc. The Gangetic plains have various types of deciduous vegetation, but no heavy forestation as such, the main forests being those of sal trees. The south has a variety of tropical vegetation, hardwood forests (such as rosewood and teak) and softwoods and bamboo. Bamboo and teak are also found in the east. The coastal areas and the Deccan abound in palms. Among India's main forest products are teak, sal, and bamboo.

At the foothills of the Himalayas, a thousand-mile belt of

lush forests called the Tarai is home to many of the animals which have inspired hunters and artists alike in India. South of the easternmost part of this belt, in the Ganges Delta, are the *Sundarbans* ("beautiful forest"), the native habitat of the awe-inspiring Bengal tiger. Other forests are also home to tigers, panthers, and assorted species of the feline family. In fact, India is the only country to have the lion *and* the tiger, although the lion is an endangered species now and only inhabits the Gir Forest National Park in Gujarat in the west of India. In addition to felines, there are hundreds of species of reptiles, including crocodiles, lizards, and snakes. Perhaps the most famous or notorious of the last is the cobra. There are also over 2,000 species of birds in India. The other wild Indian animals are elephants, rhinoceroses, antelopes, deer, bears, pigs, pandas, and wild dogs. Last, but not least, one must mention the mythical Abominable Snowman who many claim to have seen in the Himalayan snows, particularly in the higher altitudes of Sikkim. However, it is unclear if this is man or beast, and we should leave it at that!

As beautiful and exciting as India's wildlife is, it is seriously endangered. Indiscriminate hunting, poaching, and habitat elimination (due to severe deforestation) have reduced India's wildlife population considerably. Attempts are being made to rectify the situation by the creation of sanctuaries and national parks which have, fortunately, been quite successful in providing a safe haven for endangered species, enabling them to recover their numbers.

CHAPTER FOUR

What are the languages of India?

In the eighteenth century, Sir William Jones, an English scholar working in Calcutta, surprised the world by announcing that Europeans had linguistic kin living in India. He (and a few other scholars before him) were struck by the similarities between Sanskrit, the classical literary language of India, and Latin and Greek, the classical languages of Europe, and the Germanic languages. It was subsequently established that the Indo-European languages had been brought to India around 1500 B.C. by the Aryan-speaking branch of one of the Indo-European speaking tribes dispersing from southern Russia or central Asia to various parts of the world. Thus, most Indian languages belong to the Indo-Aryan group of languages which belong to the Indo-Iranian group of languages which belong to the Indo-European family of languages. Very few people are aware of this because the cultural differences between the East and the West seem so vast, but most Indian languages come from the same root as European languages and some other Asian languages such as *Farsi* (Persian). Not surprisingly, many words from these diverse cultures are almost identical.

Sanskrit was an oral heritage for many centuries. This ancient language has suffered a strange destiny. First, it was spoken only and not written; then it was written and spoken; and now it is mainly written and not commonly spoken! It is interesting that the Harappans, who lived in India around 2500 B.C., had a script (as yet undeciphered) a thousand years before the Aryans had even arrived in India. *(See Chapter Five.)* The language of the Harappans has still not been ascertained although several theories have been put forward. After the Harappans, the earliest evidence of writing in India comes from the 3rd century B.C. from one of Emperor Ashoka's edicts, which was deciphered in 1837. The deciphered script was Brahmi, the mother of all current Indian scripts except Urdu (which is a modified form of the Persian script). There are several theories about the origin of the Brahmi script, but it seems that in all probability it is of Semitic (Aramaic) derivation and was brought to India around 800-700 B.C. via the many trading routes which coexisted with civilized life in the Indian subcontinent. Another script which existed contemporaneously with Brahmi was Kharoshti, which was derived from Aramaic, but did not survive. Brahmi was the source of the scripts used for Sanskrit, the major literary language in India.

With time, many dialects called Prakrit (with which the common man felt more at ease) developed from Sanskrit. Thus, the Buddha used Prakrit for his sermons so that people from all walks of life could understand them. By the 10th century many vernaculars, including Hindi, had developed out of the interaction of Sanskrit and local dialects.

By the 12th century A.D. Turkish invaders brought *Farsi,* or Persian, into the governance of the country as a result of which many Persian words became common parlance. *Farsi* combined with Hindi was the source of *Hindustani,* which in turn became the source of Hindi and Urdu, the two main literary languages of northern India today. Hindi, influenced greatly by Sanskrit, uses the Devnagari script which is derived from Brahmi. Urdu, influenced greatly by Persian, derives its script (commonly called Urdu) from the Persian-Arabic script.

Although the script for most Indian languages comes

from Brahmi, there are four separate language families in India. As mentioned earlier, the major language group is the Indo-Aryan. There are three other language families in India. Of these the major language group is the Dravidian, which is also composed of many languages. The literary languages in the Dravidian family are Tamil, Telegu, Kannada and Malayalam; there are many minor languages as well. The Tamil language is regarded as the oldest in the Dravidian family of languages. Widely considered to be the language of the original inhabitants of India (possibly the language of the Harappans), Dravidian languages are spoken mainly in the south of India. However, the language family is not confined to India, but exists in several parts of Asia and Africa as well. Over centuries the Dravidian language family has incorporated many words from Sanskrit and other languages and vice versa.

The other two major language groups in India are the Austro-Asiatic and Sino-Tibetan languages. The Austro-Asiatic language is spoken in the eastern hills of India, and the Sino-Tibetan languages are spoken in the northeastern border areas.

These four language families, the Indo-Aryan, Dravidian, Austro-Asiatic, and Sino-Tibetan, have given birth to hundreds of languages and dialects in India. Of these the Government of India recognizes fifteen languages: Assamese, Bengali, Gujarati, Hindi, Kannada, Kashmiri, Malayalam, Marathi, Oriya, Punjabi, Sanskrit, Sindhi, Tamil, Telegu, and Urdu. However, the Government of India conducts its business in only two languages, English (which has been retained as a temporary additional official language) and Hindi. Until very recently, English was the only official language of India, and even today a preponderance of official, corporate and academic activity is conducted in the English language. It should be of interest to the reader that Americans and Indians speak English for the same reason, which is that their countries were both British colonies prior to gaining independence.

English has been a boon as a common language in India even after independence for reasons that are easy to comprehend. A multitude of languages in one country, many of which have a long and rich literary heritage, causes some problems in interstate official correspondence and educational systems. There are political ramifications as well. For example, the post-independence decision to use Hindi, primarily a north Indian language, as a national language caused much resentment among speakers of the Dravidian languages as well as some other non-Hindi speakers. Fortunately, today literature in regional languages is being encouraged. As a result, the regional languages of India are flourishing, enriching her with their diversity.

Language and its study has been a preoccupation in India for hundreds of years. Around the fourth century B.C., Panini developed a science of Indian grammar, and he along with Patanjali (variously dated from 2nd century B.C. to the 5th century A.D.) and Bhartihari (570-651) are credited with laying the foundations of philology in ancient India. The *Tolkappiyyam*, the first grammar of the Tamil language, was composed in the first centuries of the Christian era. The study of Indian languages has indeed been seriously pursued through the ages in India.

CHAPTER FIVE

What happened on the road from Indus to Independence?

A complete survey of the continuous and rich history of India is quite outside the scope of this book. However, if you are going to visit a country, you must know something about its background. Therefore, we will fly through history, as it were, and try to get some idea of the developments which have created the India of today. Appropriately, we will begin with the ancestors of India at the very dawn of civilization in the subcontinent. *(A detailed chronological sequence of historical events is given in Part Two.)*

Archaeological studies reveal that earliest man probably lived in India under half a million years ago and that India in the Stone Age was populated quite far and wide. These primitive settlements, however, did not possess the elements of a civilization in the commonly understood sense of the term, i.e., a relatively advanced level of technological and cultural development and record-keeping. According to this definition, the earliest great civilizations known to man were the Sumerian, Egyptian, Indus Valley, and Chinese civilizations. The Indus Valley Civilization developed in the northwest of India.

The Indus Valley Civilization was revealed in 1924 on an archaeological expedition led by Sir John Marshall. Just like Mesopotamia on the banks of the Tigris-Euphrates River, Egypt on the Nile River, and China on the Yellow River, the Indus Valley Civilization grew in the fertile region around the powerful but beneficent river, the Indus.

The Indus, called the *Sindh* in local languages, was named by the Greeks. This river is the source of the word

Hindu, which is what the Persians called the residents of the towns and cities around the *Sindh* River over two thousand years ago. Many years later, the word *"Indus"* would provide the English with the word "India."

Although the earliest settlements in the Indus Valley existed about 6000 years ago, the period we know as the Indus Valley Civilization spanned from approximately 2500 B.C.-1500 B.C. This period is also known as the Harappan Age, and the members of this civilization are also referred to as Harappans. Harappa and Mohenjo Daro were the largest cities found by archaeologists. The Indus Valley Civilization, or Harappan Culture, was highlighted by an extremely developed merchant, residential, and civic life.

We know now from the finds at Harappa, Mohenjo-Daro, Kali Banga, Lothal, and other sites of this vast civilization in the northwest of India that there was trade between the Indus Valley and the Mesopotamian and Egyptian civilizations. The evidence is most interesting indeed. For example, we do not know if the Harappans cooked chicken the famous *Tandoori* way, but they did eat chicken, and they did export it to Mesopotamia. It seems that the Harappans developed the techniques of breeding wild fowl and may be given the credit for introducing chickens to the Sumerians and thence to the world at large. These findings lead to some interesting questions such as "How did those chickens go all the way to Babylon?" and "What else was exported?" The discovery of Lothal, found near the gulf of Cambay on the west coast of India, gives us a possible answer to these questions. Lothal may have served as a port where very small ships were brought in through a channel. Perhaps this was how the chickens made their way to Sumerian and Babylonian kitchens. Trade must have been conducted overland as well.

Other evidence also points to trade between the Harappans and other parts of the then-known world. Standard weights and measures, common currency, beads, seals used to mark merchandise and other items, and a common script, all of which have been found at the excavations, point to widespread trade by a remarkable civilization. Harappan items have also been found in other parts of the then-known world, and items from those parts of the world (as well as other parts of India) have been found at Harappa. The Harappan script has not yet been deciphered, but probably developed out of a need to maintain business accounts as was the case in other civilizations of antiquity.

As can be imagined, prosperous trade and fertile lands led to the development of sophisticated residences and lifestyles, and the civilization extended to sites spanning hundreds of miles. The prosperity of the people living in these cities is obvious from the advanced architectural designs of their solid brick houses, which even had stairways and private toilets. These bricks were so well made that they were used four thousand years later by the British in India to lay down railroads before they discovered the Harappans and the antiquity of the bricks! There is evidence that the Harappans had domesticated several animals and cattle. Among the other discoveries at the Indus Valley Civilization sites are toys, dice (probably the first anywhere), household goods (such as pots and jars), tools, and cast bronze items.

The Indus Valley Civilization was well-populated, with the population probably running into hundreds of thousands. It seems that the Harappans had a highly evolved communal life as is evidenced by the amenities found in the excavations, such as streets (some with shops), factories, public granaries, public baths, and an advanced drainage system.

An amazing thought is that a Harappan visiting India today would not feel completely out of place and would still recognize many aspects of the life he or she lived almost five thousand years ago! For example, the beginnings of Hinduism, the major religion in India, have been detected by some in Harappan symbols and idols. On a more "this-wordly level," our visiting Harappan would recognize a great variety of the crops that were grown centuries ago such as wheat, barley, legumes, cotton, mustard, sesame seeds, dates, and melons. The Harappan would also recognize some of the carts, dishes, jewelry, and pottery presently in use. In fact, the terra-cotta or clay pottery tradition which is alive and well in India today has a continuous lineage from the Harappan times. What would really surprise our visiting Harappan is that although pottery is being made and food is being grown for many more people today, the techniques in most of the villages have not changed that much. He or she would also realize with understandable pride that the Indus Valley Civilization originated the cotton and textile industry for which India has been famous through the centuries. Thus, there is an unusual and outstanding continuity of culture from the Harappan times to the present.

From this brief synopsis of the Indus Valley Civilization, we know that the Harappans dressed well, ate well, used products from far and near, and decorated their houses with artistic objects. Very oddly, however, this civilization, which seemed to be flourishing, completely disappeared by 1500 B.C. until it was unearthed in 1924. Something disastrous happened to these ancestors of India, but not all agree that it happened overnight. Some people feel that the Indus Valley Civilization was already in decline and that the end was simply hastened by some calamity. Perhaps the calamity was over-population, catastrophic floods, or invasion. We still do not know what happened although many theories continue to be put forward, and the disappearance of the Harappans is a mystery to this day.

The disappearance of the Indus Valley Civilization occurred almost at the same time as the arrival of the Aryans in northern India. The Aryans in India were one of the tribes dispersing from south Russia or Central Asia who were called Aryan not because of their race, but because of their linguistic grouping. (*See Chapter Four.*) By about 1600 B.C., the Aryans had entered India through the Hindu Kush mountains on the northern frontier, a route which would pave the way for the many invasions India was to face in the centuries ahead.

The Aryans brought the Indo-Aryan dialect into India. As stated in Chapter Four, the Indo-Aryan group of languages is a sub-group of the Indo-Iranian group, which belongs to the Indo-European family of languages. Thus, most Indian languages as well as most European and some Asian languages belong to the same linguistic family.

After the Aryans settled down in north India, approximately in the area which would later become the Punjab, they came to be called the Vedic Aryans, for this was the time that the compilation of the Vedas, the most ancient treatises of Hindu culture, was started. The Vedas, which are compiled in Sanskrit, are critical as the main (if not entirely precise) historical clues to the history of ancient India since they also mention geographical areas and events.

As stated in Chapter Four, the Vedas were a completely oral tradition until 2500 years ago. Inflexible insistence on correct recitation has resulted in the remarkable retention of the authenticity and purity of the Vedic chants. According to experts, these chants sound pretty much today as they did hundreds of years ago. Thus we have a dependable picture of Aryan life in general. We know, for example, that the *Raja,* or chieftain, and his subjects lived in a *Grama,* or village, and took advice from their councils, the *Sabha* and the *Samiti.* It is a measure of the continuity of Indian culture that the terms *Sabha, Samiti,* and *Grama* are still in use in India in their original meaning. From the Vedas it also appears that hymns and recitations by *Brahmins* (priests) accompanied every ritual and that sacrifice was one of the most important of these rituals. Sacrifice, a major Hindu ritual even today, is another example of the unbroken continuity of Vedic culture in India.

The Aryans used to drink intoxicating beverages; in fact, the *Soma* was a sacred drink around which the most important Vedic ritual was established. The Aryans are also recognized for bringing the horse to India, for the Indo-Europeans took horses with them wherever they went. They were herdsmen who valued cattle enormously and who ate beef only on special occasions. It is more than possible that the importance of the cow in India throughout the centuries comes from the ancient status of this animal. Thus, the Aryans went to war, and liked to gamble, race horses, drink, listen to music, and dance so religion was evidently not the only thing on their mind.

Women enjoyed freedom (if not equality) during this period although this was to decline in the ensuing centuries.

They participated in social events and rituals, sometimes choosing their own husbands. In a ceremony called the *swayamvara,* which means a self-chosen husband, women garlanded the winner from gathered hopefuls invited to attend the wedding. On the other hand, there seems to be no record of any parallel ritual at which women vied with each other to be selected by a husband! It also seems that women were not excluded from intellectual endeavors, for there is a record of two women, named Gargi and Maitreyi, who seem to have engaged one of the greatest sages of that period, Yagnavalkya, in interesting philosophical discourse.

The monarch or chieftain reigned over the *panchayats,* a collection of tribal assemblies, from which he derived his authority. These *panchayats* are in existence in India today and form the infrastructure for the democratic political process. The source of power in India, it seems, has always been the village and the society, rather than a divine entity personified by the king. In general, the king was responsible mainly for temporal matters and the Brahmins for spiritual matters. Eventually, the kings and the Brahmins developed a relationship of mutual support, which enhanced the powers (temporal and spiritual) of both.

From the north of India the Aryans moved east to the fertile Gangetic Plains (created by the mighty Ganges River) and then into the peninsular part of the subcontinent. Although the Aryans eventually mixed with the indigenous peoples of India, they seem initially to have been extremely conscious of their identity and composition as a group. That is, they differentiated between themselves and the original inhabitants of India, and they also differentiated strictly between the various groups which formed their society. This differentiation rigidified with time leading eventually to the much-bemoaned caste system of India. *(See Chapter Eleven.)*

The Brahmins, their collaboration with the kings notwithstanding, managed to position themselves into an indispensable place in Indian society. Nothing could be done without the Brahmins or their incantations and interpretations, which had become even more complicated with the passage of time, and they became firmly ensconced at the top strata of a class-based society. The other castes to emerge from this ordering of society were the *Kshatriya,* or warrior, the *Vaishya,* or merchant, and the *Shudra,* or lowest caste. At the bottom of this stratification, and virtually outside it, was the lowest group most commonly known as the *untouchables*. The authority of the Brahmins was to remain intact until the 6th century B.C. when their status was questioned by several new schools of philosophy. Of these, two philosophies, one propounded by Gautama Buddha, the founder of Buddhism, and the other by Mahavira Jina, the founder of Jainism, were to influence Hinduism profoundly.

There were important developments on the Indian political front as well. Cities had begun to form in the fertile Gangetic plain, and several small kingdoms prospered. From these kingdoms the first Indian emperor, Chandragupta Maurya, emerged as the strongest. In 319 B.C. he created the Mauryan dynasty in Magadha (approximately today's Bihar). The Mauryan dynasty would last for almost 140 years.

A few years before the Mauryan dynasty was established, in about 327 B.C., Alexander the Great, hearing of India's wealth, had crossed over the northern mountain passes and arrived on India's doorstep. One of Alexander's victorious battles on his march through northwestern India was with King Porus, who ruled the banks of the Jhelum River. Alexander's encounter with the defeated King Porus is legendary, and he is reported to have treated a king, albeit a defeated one, as a king!

Alexander, called *Sikander* in India (a popular name, understandably, in the centuries to come) crossed victorious over the Punjab. After reaching the Beas River, he found that he had to retreat. It is said that Alexander himself would have gone on across India, but his troops refused to fight. Rumor has it that they were willing to tackle the armies, but the mosquitoes proved to be insurmountable! On some trips to India I have empathized with those footweary soldiers for this very reason. In any event, Alexander turned homewards although he died before he could reach home. According to some accounts, Alexander met the young Chandragupta Maurya during his stay in India, and the latter made enough of an impression that this meeting was recorded by the Greeks.

Seleucus Nikator, a general in Alexander's army, founded the Seleucid dynasty in Asia Minor after Alexander's death and brought the latter's conquered territories under his control. Seleucus' ambassador, Megesthenes, went to Chandragupta Maurya's court and remained for four years at the capital, Pataliputra (today's Patna). Megesthenes wrote *Indica*, a book on India, in which he noted with amazement that Indians lived very sophisticated and well-furnished lives under an efficient government. Taxila, a large and prosperous city of the north, had universities and medical schools. Megesthenes' book is lost now, but was used as a reference by later Greek writers who might have embellished his facts somewhat. These later books, as well as some notes made by

Alexander's entourage, made India very familiar to the Greeks.

We also get a detailed view of the Maurya administration from the *Arthashastra*, a classic book on the art and artfulness of government. *Arthashastra* was written by Kautilya (also called Chanakya and Vishnugupta) who was Chandragupta Maurya's indispensable prime minister. We know from these contemporary accounts that the Indian populace was kept well under control in districts supervised by an elaborate system of bureaucracy and spies, but that the people continued to be prosperous and industrious.

India saw a continuation of the development presaged at Harappa as she approached the end of the first millennium B.C. Trade continued, and improved, and this led to India's preeminence in the world as a source of natural resources and manufactured goods. In the centuries ahead, trade revenue would contribute to the wealth of the Indian kingdoms in the north and later in the south. These kingdoms would send emissaries far and wide to other parts of Asia, China, and Europe, and to Red Sea and Gulf ports; these emissaries would carry with them the impact of the culture they represented.

Chandragupta's grandson, called Ashoka the Great (274B.C.-232B.C.) is regarded as one of the most influential monarchs of India. Ashoka's life was changed by his violent, if victorious, battle at Kalinga (today's Orissa). He was so moved by the destruction that he devoted the rest of his life to the propagation and implementation of non-violent Buddhist principles. Ashoka sent Buddhist envoys to Syria, Macedonia, Nepal, Ceylon, and countries in Southeast Asia and is credited with making Buddhism a major religion in Asia. We still have evidence of these efforts in durable edicts in Prakrit and other languages which were carved on rocks and pillars on Ashoka's orders. One of these pillars in Sarnath had a four-headed lion capital, which the Government of India has adopted as its official emblem.

After Ashoka's conversion to Buddhism, his empire was administered under the principles of non-violence, religious tolerance, and social welfare, and it became remarkable for its humanity. Ashoka was an astute ruler, as well as a spiritual one, who saw to it that administration and revenue collection were assiduously carried out and that his subjects had duties as well as rights. By the time of his death he held sway over most of the subcontinent and had friendly ties with the kingdoms of the south.

The Mauryan Empire went into a decline following Ashoka's glorious rule. However, the powerful merchant and artisan guilds continued to grow in wealth from the sale of Indian goods prized at home and abroad. These guilds were for many centuries a prominent and continuous feature in the history of India. The fact that the popularity of Indian goods continued apace, political upheavals notwithstanding, is evident from Pliny's criticism in the first century A.D. that Rome's treasury lost millions a year in gold just because of its indulgence in luxury goods from India.

After the decline of the Mauryan dynasty, parts of north and northwest India came under the rule of Indo-Greek kings (of whom *Milinda* or Menander was the most famous) and became the venue through which the Indian and Greek cultures maintained contact. Then, around the first century B.C., the Central Asian tribe of Scythians (called *Shakas* in India) replaced the Indo-Greeks. They established their presence in the north, spread southwards, continuing as a political power until the fourth century A.D. The northern route, opened by the Aryans, was to be an oft-used passage to India.

After the Shakas, a powerful nomadic tribe, the Kushans (the Yeuh-Chih of Central Asia) came to India via Kabul in the first century A.D. They established their empire, giving India her next monarch of note, Kanishka, who was admired for his enlightened rule. The Kushans were the first Indian rulers to issue gold coins, and their prosperous empire eventually spread extensively in all four directions, covering most of central and north India, Afghanistan, and probably Central Asia. They were instrumental in spreading Buddhism to Central Asia and China, but patronized all religions. The Kushan empire lasted until the middle of the third century A.D.

In the early years of the Christian era, there was an important movement from the Deccan towards the north by the powerful and widespread Satyavahana kingdom of Andhra. The Satyavahanas were prominent in south and central India until the third century A.D. The other kingdoms in the peninsular south, as mentioned in the contemporary literature of the day, were the Cheras in the west (Kerala today), the Pandyas in the center (Tamil Nadu today), and the Cholas in the east (Tamil Nadu today). This was also the period of the short-lived but glorious rule of Kharavela in Kalinga (today's Orissa), which saw tremendous expansion and wealth.

Some of the great southern cities of two thousand years ago, such as Madurai, Kanchipuram, and Tanjore, have enjoyed the status of being centers of learning and the arts to this day. The most outstanding literary events of that time were the *Sangam (Cankam),* or poetic conferences, which produced the *Tolkapiyyam,* or Tamil grammar, as well as 2,000 poems. Fortunately, this literature has survived and gives us invaluable clues to the lives of the people at that time.

This period also saw a great deal of prosperity, and royal patronage resulted in some timeless works of art. The people lived well and enjoyed meat, wine, and other luxuries. Meanwhile, the rulers kept each other engaged in alternating alliances and battles. Like their counterparts in the north, these prosperous kingdoms had flourishing trade, first with Europe and then with the east, overseas, and inland. Treasures of Roman coins have been found in south India, bearing witness to Pliny's opinion that India was getting rich in gold while Rome was collecting peacock feathers!

In the north the dynasty of Chandra Gupta (no relation to the Mauryan emperor) took over the reins of northern India around 300. Chandra Gupta was succeeded by his son Samudra Gupta who was famous as a great conqueror. In 375, Samudra Gupta's son, Chandra Gupta II, also known as Vikramaditya, became emperor. He enjoys a Solomon-like reputation in India for his wisdom, perhaps because he continued the tradition of religious tolerance, supported intellectuals and the fine arts, and ruled in a most beneficial manner for his people and his treasury. Chandra Gupta also added to the Gupta domains and defeated the Shakas, thereby extending the Gupta Empire in the west. He made a powerful alliance when he married his daughter to King Rudrasena II of the Vakataka dynasty, which had replaced the Satyavahanas in the Deccan. The Gupta dynasty eventually extended over more than half of India from Afghanistan in the west to Burma in the east, to the Deccan in the south, and up to Kashmir in the north.

The Gupta period in Indian history was unrivaled in literature, science, art, and trade. The great poet-dramatist Kalidasa, the author of *AbhignanSakuntalam* and several other Sanskrit classics, was a member of Vikramaditya's court. A contemporary of Kalidasa was Amarsimka, the author of *Amarakosha*, a Sanskrit glossary or dictionary. Plays were popular with elite characters speaking Sanskrit, and the characters representing the common man speaking Prakrit, Sanskrit's simplified form. The cave frescoes of Ajanta were also started during this period, and the impact of Gupta art spread far and wide as evidenced by its presence in Borobodur in Indonesia, and several other places. Vikramaditya's iron pillar at Delhi stands untarnished even today, a monument to the advanced level of applied metallurgy of the Guptas. Many gold coins struck during the Gupta period have been recovered, providing further evidence of the Guptas' power and prosperity.

One of the primary sources of information for this period is Fahein, the Chinese Buddhist traveler who arrived in India in 399 and stayed for at least six years. His record is invaluable. Not only did he give posterity information about lifestyles (such as the fact that Indians were mostly vegetarians and teetotalers), but he provided a comparative international view as well. For example, he reported that Indian people of the time enjoyed great liberty and that India as a country was safe and wealthy with many large cities, hospitals, charitable institutions, and imposing structures. Not that everything Fahein found was praiseworthy. He also writes of the custom according to which a low-caste person was required to notify others, as he or she approached, in order to prevent pollution by touch. Sad to say, this belief in becoming contaminated by touching a low-caste person existed well into the twentieth century in India and is not entirely gone even today in some parts of the country.

The last two Gupta emperors were Kumara Gupta (415-454) and his son Skanda Gupta (455-467). The Gupta era of progress and prosperity in India was undermined by the incursions of the Huns (who may or may not have been connected to Attila the Hun and his hordes who terrified Europe in the sixth century). In 500 the Huns, after frequent attempts to penetrate north India, succeeded under their leader Toramana, causing the disintegration of the Gupta Empire. Toramana's son, Mihirgula, indulged in such cruelty as to become the stuff of horror stories in India.

Confusion after the Huns lasted in north India until 606, when Harsha Vardhana took control and made his capital at Kannauj (near today's Kanpur in the northern state of Uttar Pradesh). Harsha's empire would cover all but the south of India. He restored peace, security, prosperity, and the arts, for half a century, and somehow managed to find the time to write three classical plays as well. Like Chandragupta's reign, Harsha's reign is well-recorded thanks to the efforts of Huen Tsang, a visiting Chinese dignitary, and Banabhatta, a courtier, both of whom left scholarly records of the era.

In the south, from the fourth century to the ninth century, the Pallavas dominated the history of *Tamil Nad* (the land of the Tamil-speaking peoples). The Pallavas were great patrons of all religions and the arts and architecture. A maritime kingdom, they spread to Southeast Asia. Southern sea trade also carried the talents and inspiration of the Pallava artists to China and Southeast Asia. The other dynasty to rise in the south in the sixth century was that of the Chalukyas of

Badami who ended the Vakataka rule. The outstanding Chalukya monarch, Pulakeshin, defeated both of his illustrious contemporaries, Harsha Vardhana and King Mahendra Varman I of the Pallavas. The Chalukyas and the Pallavas battled for control of the South for generations, but in the ninth century, the ancient Cholas rose to prominence, and ruled Tamil Nad until the thirteenth century. The Chola period was also one of expansion overseas, as well as sophisticated government and flourishing art and architecture at home. The Cholas were replaced by the ancient Pandyas in the thirteenth century. The Pandyas brought Tamil Nad and other territories under their sway until 1311 when they were invaded by the Sultanate of Delhi. This eventually resulted in the formation of the Sultanate of Madura and by the fifteenth century Pandya territory was fragmented. *(See Part Two.)*

In the east, the Buddhist Pala dynasty ruled from the eighth to the twelfth centuries, and intermittently extended over what is now approximately Bengal, Bihar, Orissa, and Assam. A substantial portion of the north came under the rule of the Gurjara Pratiharas, who rose in the eighth century and ruled until the close of the tenth century. The Chalukyas were defeated by the Rashtrakutas whose empire then extended over western and central Deccan from the eighth to the tenth centuries. The Rashtrakutas tried unsuccessfully to advance into north India. The second line of Chalukyas took over from the Rashtrakutas in the tenth century A.D. and ruled the Deccan until the twelfth century.

It is significant that although warring factions kept the maps of India in flux during the early centuries of the second millennium A.D., trade continued unabated, and India continued to be famous as a land of wealth. Perhaps this prosperity is what made the Indians complacent. Indian princes and their subjects were busy enjoying their wealth and winning and losing battles among themselves, and it appears that they were too preoccupied to take much notice of the rest of the world. Thus, they ignored the commencement of a round of invasions from the northwest which was to lead to a marked change in life as they knew it.

By the eighth century brief attacks on the northwestern frontier of India had given Arab invaders control over areas in the Punjab and the Sindh. However, it was not until the beginning of the eleventh century that a serious invasion of India was attempted by Mahmud of Ghazni. The first of a succession of Turkish invaders, he was the first to introduce Islam into the Indian heartland through invasion. This marked the beginning of what historians would call the Muslim Period. Ghazni conducted many successful raids into India between 1001 and 1030, pillaging Hindu temples every year. He seemed to like scholarship as much as he liked plunder and was the patron of two of the greatest scholars of that period, Alberuni and Firdausi. Alberuni accompanied Ghazni and wrote an excellent detailed commentary on India. Firdausi, the great Persian poet, wrote the *Shah Nama,* a history of his time. Ghazni annexed the Punjab through his invasions, but he failed to establish a dynasty or rule.

Ghazni was followed in 1175 by Mahmud Ghori, also a Turk, who established the first Muslim Sultanate in India at Delhi, which he left in the hands of Qutbuddin Aybak, a slave who had risen to be a general.

Qutbuddin established the Slave Dynasty in Delhi in 1206, but the successors of Qutbuddin subjected their subjects to endless succession struggles and disarray until the appearance of Jalaluddin who established the Khalji (Turkish) dynasty in 1290. It was during the reign of Jalaluddin's nephew Allauddin Khalji, whose armies plundered the Deccan, that south India first felt the impact of the Muslim rulers of the north.

The Khaljis were followed by the Afghan dynasty of the Tughlaqs who were succeeded by another Afghan dynasty, the Lodis; these dynasties ruled the Sultanate for almost two centuries. These rulers established the Sultanate's control over most of India, increasing its territories and wealth.

In the meantime, the Deccan was under the control of a new set of players. To give a brief overview, the second line of Chalukyas (of Kalyani) ruled over the western and central Deccan from the tenth to the twelfth centuries when they were overthrown by the Yadavas who established their capital at Devagiri. The Yadavas were gradually overtaken by pressure from the northern Sultanate and the ascendant southern Hoysala dynasty. *(See Part Two.)* The Pandyas reigned supreme in Tamil Nad from the thirteenth century until the advent of the Delhi Sultanate. The destiny of all these southern kingdoms would soon be linked to the northern rulers when they would be incorporated into the Delhi Sultanate and then the Mughal Empire.

The Delhi Sultanate incorporated most of its southern territory under Muhammed ibn Tughlaq. The subjugated chieftains of these southern territories eventually rebelled against the Sultanate, and out of the various contenders, the kingdoms of Vijayanagar and Bahmani emerged as the most powerful in the middle of the fourteenth century. In the end, both the Vijayanagar and Bahmani kingdoms would become part of the Mughal Empire.

In spite of Muhammed Tughlaq's annexations, the reign of Feroz Shah Tughlaq (the last of the line) would see the steady disintegration of the Sultanate and the decline of power at Delhi. Feroz's death in 1388 and the decrepitude at Delhi made way for the terrible visit of Timur the Lame, the feared conqueror, to India in 1398. Timur destroyed Delhi in a frenzy of plunder and bloodshed, reducing its population to almost nothing. He did not, however, stay on to establish any political power or order. The Sultanate of Delhi managed to survive the catastrophe of Timur, and went on to play a critical part in the history of India until the arrival of the Mughals in the sixteenth century.

Even before the arrival of the Mughals, the Sultans of Delhi had contributed to the fabulous art and the architectural style which would reach its peak with the Mughals. The Sultans were great builders and left many beautiful monuments for posterity which visitors to India still enjoy. For example, Qutbuddin Aibak built the Qutb Minar, one of India's most beautiful and intriguing *minars,* or towers. The Minar, which leans a bit to the side, is one of the tallest in the world. I remember, as a child, my friends and I being quite out of breath by the time we reached the top. Now no one is allowed inside. Other monuments of this period are the Lodi Gardens, Purana Qila, and several others.

In spite of these aesthetic accomplishments, the harshness of the Sultanate's policies, the ruthless struggles of succession among the incumbents and would-be incumbents to the throne, and its perpetual wars, made the Sultanate vulnerable. At the end, the Sultanate succumbed to the next attack from the northwest, which came in the person of Babur, a direct descendent of two of the fiercest Mongol warriors ever known to mankind, Timur and Genghis Khan. Therefore, Babur's descendants would be known as *Mughals* in India.

Babur reached India in 1523 and won almost all of North India within three years. He killed Sultan Ibrahim Lodi at the Battle of Panipat, ending the Lodi dynasty, and with it the Delhi Sultanate, which he replaced with the Mughal empire. A man of word as well as sword, Babur wrote the *Tuzk-i-Baburi*, a realistic account of his adventures in and out of India. He died in 1530 and left his infant empire to his son Humayun. There is a story we were told as children about Babur's death. Humayun was deathly ill, and Babur prayed fervently that his life be taken *in lieu* of his son's life. Evidently his prayers were answered, for he died, and Humayun recovered.

Humayun did not possess the legendary Mongol martial expertise, and after two bloody battles he was defeated by Sher Khan Suri, the Afghan Sultan of Bihar and Bengal. Sher Khan then came to be known as Sher Shah Suri, and he regained the Delhi Sultanate for a brief period. An accomplished and talented ruler, Sher Shah Suri initiated reforms in administration, revenue, and currency.

Sher Shah Suri's successors fell apart after his death, and Humayun, who had been cooling his heels in Kabul, crossed the Indus and regained Delhi after twelve years of plotting and planning. Humayun then ruled for about a quarter of a century. He died after being injured in a fall and was succeeded by his son, Akbar the Great, one of the most illustrious kings of India. A study of Akbar's reign shows that he more than deserved this nomenclature. Akbar's vision, idealism and sagacious statesmanship earn him one of the highest places among the rulers of mankind.

Akbar wanted very much to be an Indian ruler in an empire in which Hindus and Muslims alike were participants. He was keenly interested in studying the principles of Islam, Hinduism, Zoroastrianism and Christianity. Although illiterate Akbar was an intent listener to the intellectual discussions of the scholars he brought to his court. Jesuit priests, Zoroastrians, and Hindu scholars were invited to his court, and they translated the New Testament and Sanskrit masterpieces (among other religious works) into Persian. Akbar founded the *Din-i-Illahi*, a system of beliefs in which he incorporated what he felt was the best that all the religions of the world had to offer. Needless to say, Akbar's eclectic religious style did not sit well with all of his subjects, and there was criticism and resentment against his open-mindedness. However, his administrative success and personal authority prevented any public display of disapproval.

In a predominantly Hindu country with a Muslim rulership, Akbar judiciously implemented his eclectic beliefs. Unlike his predecessors, he included Hindus in his administration, appointed Hindus to prominent positions as generals and ministers, and reformed discriminatory laws. He married Rajput Hindu princesses from Rajasthan, one of whom produced his son and heir, Prince Salim, or, as he was known after his succession, Jehangir. In short, Akbar employed every policy which moved toward the objective of forging a harmonious and productive society.

Akbar's success was partly due to the fact that his empire was a study in organization. He divided his empire into a system of administrative units which lasted well beyond the Mughals. Likewise, Akbar's army was organized on a hierarchical pattern which produced very successful campaigns and which would also last for centuries after him. He was a great builder. Akbar's architectural contributions include the forts at Agra, and Fatehpur Sikri, Humayun's tomb, and other monuments.

Akbar expanded the Mughal Empire to include Qandhar, Baluchistan, Sindh, Gujarat, Bihar, Bengal, Kashmir, Orissa, and the Deccan. It was arguably one of the most powerful and prestigious empires of its time. His subjects were generally happy and his treasury was full. Records of Akbar's reign are available to us via Abul Fazl's *Ain-i-Akbari* and *Akbarnama*.

Akbar was succeeded in 1605 by his son, Jehangir, a romantic figure in legend if not in reality. Jehangir followed his father's style of tolerant ruling by and large, but seems to have been overly influenced by his beloved wife, Mehrunnisa, a lady of the Mughal court, whom he renamed Nur Jehan. An active political player who liked to be in control, she became a power to be reckoned with at the Emperor's court. She arranged for her niece Arjumand Bano Begum to marry Jehangir's third son, Prince Khurram, who became the future Mughal Emperor Shah Jehan. Nur Jehan eventually retired from politics when Shah Jehan became emperor.

Shah Jehan was mainly tolerant, and like his father and grandfather gave patronage to all groups of subjects. The world would know him best, however, for the love he bore for his wife, Arjumand Bano Begum, whom he renamed Mumtaz Mahal. She died in childbirth, but would be immortalized throughout the world and for eternity as the inspiration for the Taj Mahal, a tomb built by her ardent and grieving husband. One of the most successful examples of international collaboration, started in 1632, the Taj Mahal was designed by an Indian, a Frenchman, and an Italian. Three years earlier,

Shah Jehan had commissioned the legendary and fabulously bejeweled Peacock Throne. This throne was taken to Iran in 1739 by Nadir Shah where its reproductions seated Iranian royalty. It is possible that one of the jewels from the original Peacock Throne might have been the Koh-i-noor or "mountain of light," which, along with other jewels taken from India, is part of the Crown Jewels of Britain. A prolific builder, Shah Jehan also ordered the construction of the Red Fort, Jama *Masjid* (Mosque), and other timeless landmarks in India.

The aura of greatness which the Mughal Empire acquired began to evaporate when Shah Jehan's son, Aurangzeb, ascended the throne in 1657. Aurangzeb proved to be quite different from his enlightened forefathers. Among the many strange and cruel acts of his rule were the murders of his brothers and the incarceration unto death of his father, son and daughter.

Aurangzeb's oppressive policies caused great rebellion and unrest. He was an orthodox Muslim who persecuted Hindus, and the Muslim sects of *Shias* and *Sufis* alike. Unlike others from his family, Aurangzeb did not patronize the arts. Rather, he destroyed schools and temples, seeing all these institutions as incongruous with his religious beliefs. Ironically, he lived an austere life and supposedly earned his daily bread by handstitching caps.

Aurangzeb did not allow his asceticism to prevent him from expanding the Mughal empire prodigiously from Afghanistan to the Burmese border and from Kashmir to Hyderabad. However, keeping the Deccan under control was not easy, and Aurangzeb's ongoing attempts to subjugate the Deccan became a sore which would bleed him of men, money, and morale. Although he increased the size of the Mughal empire to the maximum, the growth was only in area. Aurangzeb was never able to provide the political leadership which would cement his conquests. (*See Part Two.*)

One of the main reasons for Aurangzeb's inability to incorporate the south successfully into the Mughal Empire was that the Marathas had by this time established themselves as a powerful force in the Deccan. The Hindu Marathas were united by religious fervor, and by their political and cultural values, and this unity was critical to their rise as a dominant force in the Deccan.

The Marathas first rallied under Shahuji Bhonsle and then under his more famous son, Sivaji Bhonsle. Although Shahuji was a leader, Sivaji's mother generally gets the credit for raising a hero. Sivaji was the first Indian on record to raise the cry for *Swarajya,* or self rule, a cry that would be heard all over India in the twentieth century as the country struggled for the independence which she enjoys today. Using guerrilla tactics and a large following of willing soldiers who revered him as a semi-divine leader, Sivaji soon found himself in charge of the Maratha homeland and beyond. His rise to power was funded by his constant raids on Mughal possessions. Sivaji's brutal murder of General Afzal Khan of Bijapur (one of the former Bahmani states) established the Marathas as the predominant force in the Deccan. Sivaji seemed to have been very concerned about the European presence on the western coast and built naval fortresses for the defense of his territories.

Sivaji's daring adventures and escapes (including one in a basket from Aurangzeb's "hospitality") are narrated even today in India. He was crowned *Chhatrapati* (King) in 1674 at a traditional ceremony in Raigarh where he received allegiance from the Marathas. His son Sambhaji was not made of the same mettle as his father. Sambhaji rebelled against his father and joined his enemies. When Sivaji died, Sambhaji found he was no match for the Mughals. At this point Aurangzeb enters our story again, this time because he ordered the literal butchering of Sambhaji. The humiliation of Sambhaji's gruesome death served the purpose of uniting the Marathas, and thereafter they rallied against the Mughals with even greater fervor. The eventual crowning of Sivaji's grandson Shahuji and his restoration organized the Marathas under the leadership of the Peshwas (hereditary Prime Ministers). The Peshwas provided a focal point for the various Maratha clans i.e., the Sindhias, Gaekwads, Holkars, and Bhonsles, who fought together, first as a single force and then as a confederacy.

Aurangzeb died in 1707, and judging from his own writings, he died a sad and confused person. He was buried in Daulatabad, a small town near today's Aurangabad in the south of India. His son, Bahadur Shah, then ruled until 1712, but the Mughal heyday was over. The successors of Aurangzeb all turned out to be weak, decadent, and utterly incapable of carrying the powerful mantle of their predecessors.

Although the Mughals played a critical role in the kingdoms of the Deccan, they were unsuccessful in subjugating the entire south of India. In fact, a look at the map of India throughout the Ashokan, Gupta, and Mughal reigns shows that the southernmost tip of the country was never completely controlled by any of these great empires. The south was not the only area out of the control of the Mughals. In fact by the dawn of the eighteenth century the entire Mughal empire had collapsed. The Mughal court, which had once inspired awe and fear, was now a powerless center of indulgence and ineptitude. The time was ripe for another rapacious visitor to appear on the scene from the north.

In 1739 Nadir Shah, ruler of Persia, invaded India. Like other plunderers before him, he left massacred Indians and emptied treasuries behind, but he did not establish a stronghold in Delhi. Sadly, if predictably, the descendants of the great Mughals were unable to seize the political opportunity hidden under the debris and confusion in Delhi and to turn it to their advantage.

In the meanwhile, in spite of her changing political fortunes, India continued to be one of the leading manufacturing countries in the world, a fact recorded by many travelers of the sixteenth and seventeenth centuries. The ports of India were famous for trade as well as for shipbuilding, and legends of the wealth of India traveled as far and wide as the goods it produced and beyond. However, this would change by the eighteenth century, when India's wealth would be controlled by Europe.

By the fifteenth century, Europe, having become well-informed about the wealth of India, had already sent her traders. These Europeans set sail for India, disembarked on her shores, settled down with profit on their minds, and made no immediate plans to leave. First the Portuguese traders arrived, followed by the Dutch, the English, then the French, and all of them were soon fighting each other over their "possessions" in a foreign land. These skirmishes would end with the eventual success of the British over the other European nations in India and ultimately with the subjection of India to

British colonialism. But first, let us quickly go over the events which would lead to that event.

The first Portuguese ship to reach India brought Vasco da Gama to Calicut in 1498 where he was warmly welcomed by the *Zamorin,* or prince, who exchanged gifts with the new arrivals. However, the Portuguese had more in mind than the exchange of gifts, namely, trade, and the propagation of Catholicism. Da Gama went back to Portugal, and within two years he returned fully armed for negotiating strength. Soon Goa was settled as an outpost of the Portuguese empire. By 1511, the Portuguese were in control of Goa which was mostly Catholic, prosperous, and on record as being an object of contemporary admiration.

Portugal was annexed to Spain in 1580, and the defeat of the Spanish Armada in 1588 encouraged the Dutch and the English to go where the Portuguese had gone. In fact, the same rumors of the treasures and spices of the "Indies" which lured Alexander to India in 327 B.C. were whetting the appetites of Western sailors and navigators almost two millennia later. Ships with less capable navigators went in the opposite direction, made landfall in the West, and mistakenly thought that they had reached India. This is why the peoples of the Americas would find themselves being called Indians!

At any rate, the Dutch and the English also finally arrived in India, threatening Portuguese control. The intolerance of the Catholic Portuguese had already caused them to become seriously unpopular. One of the most compelling sources of this contention was the fact that the Portuguese controlled the sea routes used by Muslims going to Mecca on the Haj pilgrimage. Since this centuries-old pilgrimage is the most important journey a Muslim can undertake, such control and resultant interference created tremendous resentment. Portuguese strength on the Arabian Sea and the Indian Ocean would change with the arrival of the English.

The English East India Company was established in 1600 as a private venture with an investment of 50,000 English pounds. The first Company representative arrived in India in 1608 with gold and a letter from King James I for Emperor Jehangir, but he was not given an audience. Mughal indifference to the English continued until 1612 when the English defeated the hated Portuguese ships. The Company had not envisioned a future for itself as a naval arm for the Mughal empire. However, the naval capability displayed by the English certainly impressed the mighty, but non-maritime, Mughals. It goes to the credit of the Company that when it saw that its job description in India could entail more than just conducting trade, it had the acumen to seize the opportunity. In 1615 Sir Thomas Roe was received with honor at the Mughal *durbar* (court) and subsequently allowed to establish factories at Surat, Ahmedabad, and Cambay. This was the first step taken by the English towards setting up unbelievably profitable trade and other agreements with local rulers in India. The rest, as they say, is history!

For the English as well as for the other Europeans at this time, trade was the name of the game in India. There was, however, more than a slight problem for the Europeans in fulfilling this desire for international trade. The fact was that the Europeans lacked resources to exchange and as mercantilist nations, they did not want to part with bullion. On the other hand the only European exchange items the Indians thought worth having at the time was gold or silver. The problem was solved by the Europeans by the establishment of an elaborate system of trade by exchange which basically tried to keep European silver at home. Thus, from Madras and Gujarat the Europeans acquired cotton; from Gujarat they acquired indigo; from Bengal they acquired silk, sugar, and saltpeter; and from Malabar they acquired spices. The European traders then exchanged these Indian goods with goods and spices from countries farther east, for much less than what they would have paid for them had they gone directly to the "Spice Islands" of the East Indies. Interestingly, India's love for gold and silver, would, after almost fifteen centuries, cause consternation all over again in Europe. (Things truly do not change that rapidly in India. Even today Indians prize gold jewelry above all other personal items.)

This multi-exchange European trade system would take many forms. Later, when Chinese tea became a habit in Europe, the British illegally traded opium from Bengal for Chinese tea. Opium was contraband in China, but in spite of this fact, British traders pursued the illegal opium trade relentlessly because it enabled them to carry on the ever-expanding Anglo-Chinese tea trade without paying in bullion. China's objection to the British pushing Indian opium on the Chinese, and the devastating effects of the drug, would lead to the Opium Wars in which China would lose to Britain.

Within a short span of time, it became very obvious from the vast profits made by the European traders, that India had fully lived up to its reputation as a gold mine. The European traders dug in their heels, wresting trading privileges from the native rulers by force and by persuasion. Sadly, not one Indian ruler of the time appreciated the threat that had arrived on the Malabar coast in the persons of European tradesmen. The Europeans, though, had fully perceived weakness among the Indian rulers, and decided it would be more profitable to be a hated foe than an honored guest. Thus, the English East India Company, taking no chances, built forts in Calcutta, Madras, and Bombay in order to safeguard its interests. By the time of the death of Aurangzeb in 1707 the British had already acquired quite a few of the advantages and had learned several of the tricks which would eventually enable them to replace their Indian hosts as the supreme authority in the land.

The Dutch had also arrived in India with the English, but since their interests lay farther east in the Spice Islands of Southeast Asia (mainly Indonesia) they did not set up major establishments in India. The unbelievable commercial success of the Portuguese, the English, and the Dutch, inspired other countries. The French gained a foothold but no great measure of commercial success. The Danish, Austrians, Swedes, and Prussians also tried their hand at the same game, but they did not succeed for various reasons. In the end, the English, who had come to India with no desire for conquest, emerged triumphant in the bid for the goods in India, and thereafter in the quest for India herself.

The triumph of the British was heralded by their elimination of the only serious European competitor remaining in India, i.e., the French. This feat was accomplished in 1751 by Robert Clive, a young employee of the British East India Company. Clive annexed the Carnatic, putting an end to the French presence in India and establishing the British as the only European power in India. The next event in Clive's meteoric career was the horror of the "Black Hole" of Calcutta in Bengal. In 1756 Sirajuddaulah, the Nawab of Bengal attacked and captured Fort St. William. During the attack the

Nawab's men imprisoned about a hundred English men and women in an underground cellar at the Fort (which was used as a lock-up by the British). Most of those imprisoned died of shock and suffocation, creating fear among the British about the "savagery" of Indians. Clive brought Bengal under his control in 1757 after the Battle of Plassey, and replaced the Nawab with a puppet ruler named Mir Jafar. Clive became the Governor of Bengal in 1758, but left for Britain soon thereafter. His departure signaled a descent into chaos and corruption by Mir Jafar and the Company employees.

Mir Jafar was soon unable to make the heavy revenue payments he had promised to the British East India Company. He was duly replaced by Mir Qasim, who could not deliver as promised either and who fled Calcutta. Mir Qasim then returned, fortified by the presence of the Nawab of Oudh and the Mughal Emperor; all three allies were defeated by the British at Buxar. Meanwhile, the confusion in Calcutta worsened, and Clive returned in 1765 to restore order. Clive then acquired an unbelievable concession from the defeated Mughal Emperor Shah Alam II when the latter granted him a *Diwani*, or perpetual title of revenue authority over Bengal and Bihar. Now Clive was able to act as the representative of the Mughal Emperor and collect revenue (which meant in effect to rule) over a substantial part of northeastern India, which he did through an appointed Deputy *Diwan*. The die was now cast irrevocably in favor of the British by the Mughal emperor himself. Clive laid the first foundation stone of British rule in India, and upon this foundation the edifice of the empire would be built, stone by stone.

Clive did try to bring about order in Bengal by implementing administrative reforms and by regularizing business procedures and salaries in the Company. However, the greed of the company employees had entrenched a system of corruption and nepotism which was necessitated by their indulgent lifestyles. Clive perfectly symbolized this greed, for he suddenly acquired such astounding wealth that it eventually brought the wrath of the British Parliament upon him.

By 1767 there was even more trouble in east India. The Company still could not pay its promised tax of almost half a million pounds to the Treasury back home. The local populace under the Company's jurisdiction endured unrelenting and ruthless revenue collection due to insatiable Company corruption. This was the beginning of the economic exploitation of India which was to last for almost two centuries, furthering British interests while India suffered. In the midst of this debacle Clive went back to Britain, never to return to India. In 1772 Clive successfully countered charges brought against him in the British Parliament, but in 1774 he committed suicide.

The success of the British in India continued undeterred by the exit of the man history would call "Clive of India." Britain's unity of purpose, which at this time was profitable trade, remained unshaken. This unity would stand the British in good stead even in the centuries ahead when their purposes would change somewhat. British unity, superior soldiery, and weaponry, combined with divided Indians, prepared fertile ground for the planting of the seeds of the British Empire. Soon enough India found herself under the hegemony of another foreign race, culture, and *Raj*, or rule.

The British *Raj* did not appear overnight, and the British did encounter some obstacles on the road to empire. One of these obstacles, the Marathas, continued to become stronger under various Peshwas through the eighteenth century. Peshwa Balaji Vishwanath became the mentor for Shahuji, grandson of Sivaji, and guided him back to the position that his grandfather had won. Peshwa Balaji Baji Rao succeeded his father, Balaji Vishwanath, and it was thanks to the former's leadership that by the middle of the eighteenth century the Maratha chieftains were in control from Lahore in the northwest to Orissa in the East and from Delhi in the north to the Deccan. In effect, most of the country was under the leadership of the Peshwa, including the Mughal Emperor who was reduced to a figurehead in Delhi.

It seemed that Sivaji's dreams had been realized and a Maratha empire encompassing the entire country seemed very possible. However, Maratha control was shattered in 1761 when the Marathas were devastated at Panipat by the invading Afghan General Ahmed Shah Abdali. The Maratha confederacy recovered under Peshwa Madhav Rao, but it would never be its daunting self again, although it continued to challenge the British well into the first two decades of the nineteenth century. Maratha success floundered on the heels of the mutual distrust which had been present, albeit in a more dormant state, throughout the Maratha history. By the early nineteenth century the Maratha power was finished. After the Maratha collapse, the country fell into a period marked by chaos and the absence of any single powerful authority. *(See Part Two.)*

The Marathas were not the only obstacle to British victory. In the second half of the eighteenth century, the Deccan saw the rise of Hyder Ali and after him, his son Tipu Sultan. Both father and son were impassioned with the desire to throw off the growing foreign presence in India, and they were cognizant of the dire need for a concerted effort to achieve this end. Their appeals for nationalism and unity were ignored by their self-serving countrymen, and the two fell due to the treacherous behavior of other Indian rulers and the opportunism of everyone else. The only other possible remaining threat to the British was the Sikh Kingdom in the Punjab. The Sikhs under Maharaja Ranjit Singh were a formidable force, but after the Maharaja's death in 1839 and the subsequent disarray among his successors, the Sikhs succumbed to British power as well.

By the middle of the nineteenth century, all her resistance crushed, India found herself under the complete control of the British East India Company. India was no longer a place to send daredevil Englishmen who could not make their way at home. It was now a desirable career for scions of "good" families who hoped to become rulers and administrators. The successors of Clive made and unmade princes and treaties until India, incapable of defending herself, was subjugated.

After Clive, a succession of governors, then governors general, and finally viceroys, ruled parts and then all of India. Under the soldiers of the British army and then the British government itself, the British national interest was kept well-fed while that of India was gradually depleted without replenishment in any form. Having come to India for its ancient riches, Britain found new ones as well, and these riches propelled her into the ranks of the wealthiest countries in the history of the world. India herself was soon straggling, deprived in education, industry, food, and the root of it all, any control of her fortunes.

How did this happen? The main reason is quite obviously the inability of the Indian people to rise in unison to meet the challenge. There had been many invasions and incursions in the past, but the plunderers came and went, and those who conquered stayed on, made India their homeland, and did not repatriate their earnings. To meet Britain was a new challenge which required unity, but in the face of tribal, caste, religious, and regional rivalries and the absence of a common political loyalty, such unity was an impossible goal to achieve.

The British seemed to be completely in charge of their situation in India. Actually, all was not so snug under the empire's powerful blanket. Growing arrogance and the not-so-hidden racial disdain of the British for the Indians had slowly alienated both the elite and the common man in India from their British rulers. The British now looked down upon anything traditionally Indian, a far cry from their behavior as tradesmen who had deemed it an honor to be invited to the courts of the Mughals and the other princes of the land. Most sections of Indian society felt humiliated by the British and resentful of them.

Even those sections of society which had traditionally commanded respect due to Indian learning and culture were undermined by the Westernizing air that was blowing across the land. The dislocation of traditional class structures due to British land revenue settlements and the resultant dispossession and upheaval among Indians caused tremendous economic imbalance. The old order had yielded to flux, fear, and insecurity, creating the feeling that India was going to be destroyed; rebellion was now only a matter of time.

This rebellion came in the form of the Revolt of 1857-59, variously called the Indian Mutiny or the Sepoy (from *sipahi*, or soldier) Mutiny or the First War of Independence. The situation was already inflammable under the oppressive British rule, and it required but one light to start the conflagration. This light came from the violation of the religious beliefs of the Hindus (for whom beef was sacrilegious) and the Muslims (for whom pork was defiling). Indian sepoys were asked to bite open cartridges which had been greased with pork and beef before loading them into Enfield rifles. This proved to be the proverbial last straw for an indignant nation. The first insurgency of sepoys erupted in Meerut where sepoys refused orders and were imprisoned by the British. Other sepoys freed their imprisoned comrades and proceeded to kill some of the British officers. The rebellion then ignited uprisings in other areas in the north of India. The rebels reached the nominal Mughal Emperor Bahadur Shah II in Delhi, and made him their leader. A mere symbol of the tattered empire, the Emperor reluctantly found himself at the head of the Mutiny.

The British were taken by surprise, but managed to put down the Mutiny with a force and cruelty which were well reciprocated by the Indians. A period of punishment followed for India during which mutinous leaders such Tantia Topi were killed while others such as Nana Sahib, son of the last Peshwa, simply disappeared. These brave patriots are fondly remembered and celebrated in India where poignant stories about them are narrated to this day. One story tells how the Rani Laxmibai, Queen of Jhansi, died on horseback on the battlefield fighting to the last and how her infant son and heir, strapped to her back, died with her. Bahadur Shah II, the Mughal Emperor, surrendered and was deported to Burma where, homesick and heartbroken, he wrote nostalgic poetry (still recited in India) until he died in 1858.

Acts of terror against the impudent "natives" continued until order was restored in 1859. The army was now re-organized, but the loyalty of Indians, sepoy or civil, was no longer a given. It was thought important that there be fewer sepoys per each British officer and that the officers remain more in tune with their men, if only to keep their ear to the ground. The relationship of the British and the Indians was now heavy with racial implications, and society was completely polarized from this time forward. The British had prevailed, but nothing would ever again be the same for India *or* her foreign rulers.

A look at a map of India from 1858 shows that all of India was under the British either directly or indirectly. The Indians seemed to have lost everything, and the British had gained a *Raj* over India. However, something else had come to pass. All the events of the Mutiny would engender the first flames of Indian patriotism. Not many had taken notice, but, helped by stories of patriotism and sacrifice, the birth of Indian nationalism had taken place. Though the infant was small and endangered, it would survive and grow to full maturity. Some Western-educated Indians, particularly those dependent on the British for their prosperity and lifestyles, still felt very loyal to Britain and to the values exemplified by British society, but they were in a minority.

After the proclamation of British victory over the Mutiny, the Crown passed the Government of India Act of 1858 which completed the transfer of power from the British East India Company to the Crown. India was not a business venture any more; it was a proven colonial gold mine, and too much was at stake. Queen Victoria became "Empress of India" in 1876, and Lord Canning, India's Governor General, became her first Viceroy, or deputy, in India. At this stage a period of autocratic and inhumane rule was imposed on India which was justified by the British on the basis of the mutiny. As time went by, this oppression became worse; nevertheless, some sections of Indian society still remained loyal to the Crown.

Lord Canning was followed by several other Viceroys. (*See Part Two.*) However, it was Lord Lytton who was to stir up trouble for Her Majesty by passing the Vernacular Press Act of 1878. The Vernacular Press Act restricted the expression of popular opinion in vernacular papers, thus shocking the sensibilities of Indian Western-educated leaders. It seemed to these heretofore loyal Indians that while the British Crown had brought the venerable institutions of the press (and printing) to India, it was not prepared to share the venerable institution of the *free* press with its Indian subjects. Lytton also removed duties from British goods, depriving India of critically needed funds during a time of economic crisis and famine and placing British business interests above the survival of Indians.

The Vernacular Press Act was repealed after 1880 by the new and popular Viceroy Lord Ripon, who also tried to introduce reforms in representative institutions at the local level. He introduced the Ilbert Bill in 1883, which allowed Indian judges to rule in cases involving Europeans. This bill almost led to a mutiny among the British until it was abandoned, but the white supremacism prevalent among the rulers of a dark subcontinent had been exposed in all its ugliness. The good news about the failure of the Ilbert Bill was that it taught young Indian nationalists that in the face of protest the mighty *Raj* would eat its words. Two years later the Indian National Congress, India's first national political party, would hold its first meeting.

Several other events were taking place in the second half

of the nineteenth century which would shape the future of India. One of the most important of these was the development of a vast network of railways, started in 1850, which seemed to be a beacon of progress. In effect, though, the railways worked as another instrument for the rapid deployment of British troops and the harnessing and exploitation of India's resources for the benefit of Britain and the detriment of India. Cheap manufactured goods arrived in quick succession from Britain and consequently sounded the death knell for India's ancient handicraft and cottage industries. The railway did facilitate the development of some Indian industries, such as coal, iron, steel, and jute. However, all of these industries served Britain. Interestingly, the railways may also have served the national movement by quick transportation of Indians from different regions, freeing them from provincial boundaries, unifying them by cross-country participation and involvement.

Agriculture was also abused for commercial purposes by the British. The Civil War in the United States from 1861-1865 created a high demand for cotton, and Indian farmers were persuaded to change from food production to commercial agricultural production. Other farmers were encouraged to raise opium rather than food. Consequently, when the market crashed following the end of the American Civil War, there was a devastating shortage of food in India. Thus, the British agricultural policies, which only kept the British national interest in mind, caused the most ravaging famines in the entire history of the subcontinent and left Indian agriculture in a desperate state for decades thereafter.

All the developments outlined above fostered a sense of economic deprivation, exploitation, and cultural oppression which, when added to post-mutiny antagonism towards the rulers, created the new Indian nationalistic consciousness. Western-educated Indians, who were appalled by the flagrant violations of cherished British ideals in India (such as the rule of law), became leaders and acted as catalysts for the freedom movement. It was obvious to most Indians that their plight was directly attributable to their British rulers and that the British could not be relied upon to relinquish their power without some persuasion. This task of persuasion was performed by the national movement and its leaders.

The leaders of the national movement had different styles and backgrounds, but by the beginning of the twentieth century they were all moving towards one unshakable goal, i.e., freedom and independence. Some were in a hurry, while others wanted to use traditional British political processes to reach these goals. These differences in approach created two groups of nationalists, called the Moderates and the Extremists; Gopal Krishna Gokhale would lead the Moderates, and Bal Gangadhar Tilak would lead the Extremists. There were other groups and associations as well, but in time, most of these groups would come under one umbrella, the Indian National Congress (still the main political party in India today, albeit in a somewhat altered state).

The Congress had its beginnings in 1885 when it was first convened at Calcutta under the auspices of Allen Octavian Hume with Womesh C. Bonnerjee as President. At that time it was a gathering of educated, upper-class Indians who wanted to improve the condition of their countrymen by working loyally within the framework of the British constitution. This attitude of loyalty changed in time due to many factors, not the least of which was the shortsightedness of the

Viceroy Lord Curzon, an administrator without much political capability. In 1905 he partitioned Bengal into Muslim and Hindu areas in the interests of efficiency and caused havoc among all communities involved in the dismemberment of that state.

After this unfortunate administrative act was carried out by Lord Curzon, many more disillusioned Indians joined the freedom movement, which now acquired a heightened emotional flavor. This flavor was reinforced by the selection of an anthem, *Bande Mataram* (Hail Motherland), the words of which came from a novel by Bankim Chandra Chatterjee and the music for which was composed by India's unofficial national poet, Rabindranath Tagore. Indians now protested by calling for *Swadeshi*, which meant in theory "everything from our homeland." In practice this meant the boycott of British goods and services, and wearing homespun cloth while the finest British silken vanities were thrown into bonfires. *Swadeshi* spread as an ideal and as an economic movement in Bengal and thence to other parts of India. This also was the time that terrorism found favor among many Indians who were becoming tired of unsuccessful peaceful protests. By 1907 there was an irreconcilable difference of opinion about the method of protest between the Moderate and the Extremist wings of the Congress. (These two wings would be reconciled in 1916.) Mass demonstrations also became widespread now, but as yet there was no single leader of national stature.

The *Swadeshi* movement caused a ferment in Indian life in spheres other than politics. Indians started to look to themselves for movement and progress in other fields such as social reform and education. Tilak, the national leader of the Extremist group in Congress, relied on the revival of Hindu festivals and looked to India's glorious past to awaken dormant self-esteem and confidence among Indians. He created the slogan "Swarajya is my birthright, and I shall have it." Hindus who had been under non-Hindu rulers for centuries responded to Tilak with great fervor.

The Muslim national leaders could not identify with the Hindu aspect of Tilak's political ideas and worried about being a minority in a primarily Hindu country. In time this alienation would lead to the separatist movement for Pakistan although most Muslims did not join the movement. The Muslim leaders became concerned about the future prospects of Muslims and formed the All-India Muslim League in 1906, giving public expression to a separateness that they felt had been in existence for quite some time. The League sent a deputation to meet Lord Minto, the Viceroy, to request that the interests of Muslims be heeded in any constitutional reform action taken by the Crown. When the Morley-Minto Reforms were enacted as the Indian Councils Act of 1909, the Muslims were given separate electorates (*See Part Two.*)

The Act of 1909 had other repercussions as well. The British Government had begun to react to the national movement and its leaders' demands, but this response was very faint at first. Attempts had been made earlier through the Indian Councils Acts to establish some form of participation for Indians in the governmental process, but these attempts were painfully slow and at best resulted in nominal Indian participation. Indians could still be overridden, and the membership on the Councils did not give Indians power to change anything. It was John Morley who took the first step in letting Indians into their own government through elected representatives by the passage of the Indian Councils Act of 1909, even though the electorate was still not based on Universal Adult Suffrage. (*See Part Two.*)

In another effort to soothe the political ferment created by the growing success of the Indian freedom movement, the partition of Bengal was revoked by King George V at his Coronation *Durbar* (or Court) in Delhi in 1911. This caused great disappointment among the Muslims who had found themselves in a majority in some areas as a result of the partition. Thus, the problem in Bengal continued in one way or another, and unrest spread deeper and wider throughout the rest of India as the freedom movement gathered momentum. There was still no single leader, but this was soon to change when a new personality arrived on the scene in 1915. This new arrival was Mohandas Karamchand Gandhi, who had just successfully employed his strategy of Passive Resistance in South Africa. In Natal, South Africa, Gandhi led the large Indian community in its struggle against legally sanctioned racial segregation and discrimination. (*See Part Two: Year 1830)*

Gandhi had studied law in Britain, but entered politics as a reaction to the oppressive racism of the British Government in South Africa where he worked as a lawyer. This struggle against racism eventually brought Gandhi back to India where his unique political philosophy united the masses of India in a non-violent struggle for freedom. Gandhi was called "half-naked" and a "seditious *faqir* (mendicant or almsman)" by Sir Winston Churchill, but the Mahatma (or "great soul") had a sense of humor about his comparative lack of apparel. His mind was on higher things as he kept his sights on the liberation of his people. In the end, "*Bapu,*" or "Father," as Gandhi was called, would force the mighty British Empire to its knees without armed rebellion.

It is difficult to imagine the course of events in India if Gandhi had not appeared on the scene with his solutions when he did. At first glance it appears that he was leaning on ancient Hindu texts to appeal to Indians in order to resuscitate them. On closer inspection, however, it becomes obvious that he also used universally-accepted philosophical means to achieve political goals. To Gandhi the means were as important as the end. Though the end of the struggle in India was political freedom, the means had to be non-violent in nature, otherwise, violence would beget more violence. Non-violence was the cornerstone of Gandhi's philosophy. He believed in non-violent political activism in the form of non-cooperation, civil disobedience (also called passive resistance), boycott, and *sarvodaya* (self-reliance and upliftment). Non-violence could only be achieved through discipline of the mind and body. The essential ingredients of discipline were asceticism, penance, fasting, poverty, chastity, and meditation. Only when all these aspects were in place in a person's life, could he or she be an effective *satyagrahi,* or a truth crusader. Gandhi practiced even more than he preached and soon became India's favorite leader with the masses rushing forth to follow his example in part, if not wholly. The national movement in India had been progressing in fits and starts, but under Gandhi it soon snowballed to a national level. Now, for the first time, the masses were mobilizing behind *one* leader. Things were just starting to heat up at home and abroad. World War I was only a couple of years away.

When the war came, its announcement by the British government brought support from all corners of India. Men, materials and money were gathered by Indian leaders for the British war with the rationale that this unstinting support would be recognized and rewarded in the form of self-government for Indians. As a result of this cooperation, a million Indians (of whom large numbers suffered casualties) and hundreds of millions of British pounds in cash and kind went from India towards the British cause in the war.

As India united to support Britain abroad, she was becoming more and more divided at home, and divisive forces were becoming increasingly powerful. Muhammed Ali Jinnah, a close associate of the eminent Indian leader Dadabhai Naoroji and a member of the Congress, was initially as much a part of the national movement for freedom as any one of the other leaders. However, with the passage of time he too felt that the Congress, which represented a predominantly Hindu following, could not represent the Muslims of India. Thus Jinnah joined the Muslim League in 1913. The Muslims, though, were not one solid bloc and did not all follow the League platform, being variously affiliated with several parties including the Congress. For a while Jinnah worked towards cooperation with the Congress and towards Hindu-Muslim solidarity. For several years he was an important member of the Congress as well as the League. However, with enough time and rhetoric, there was open and increasing disaffection between the Muslims and the Hindus and alienation between the Congress and the League. (*See Part Two.*) Except for a short period in 1916, when the League and the Congress worked in harmony towards constitutional reform after the Lucknow Pact, Jinnah and the Congress went their very separate ways.

When World War I was over, Britain emerged victorious, but India suffered a series of setbacks. Far from receiving gratitude from the British for India's contribution to the war effort, the Indians received the Rowlatt Act of 1919. The

Rowlatt Act suppressed free speech and expression in India, causing shock and outrage to *all* Indians. Gandhi organized a disobedience movement against the Act, and was arrested in the Punjab where the unrest was the greatest. Half of the Indian soldiers of the British army were loyal Sikh soldiers and it was too much for them to revert to an oppressed condition after having fought so valiantly for the British. Discontent among the Sikhs had found expression earlier when some Sikhs had formed the revolutionary Ghadar Party in 1913 in the United States of America. Bengal continued to be unhappy. To make matters much worse, a deadly influenza epidemic struck at that time, leaving many hundreds of thousands of fatalities in its wake. The nation was staggering from a post-war depression.

It was against this background of political, social, and personal desperation that the Jallianwalla Bagh massacre occurred in 1919, horrifying the few Indians left who might have been loyal to the British. A gathering of ten thousand unarmed Indians, including women and children, had collected at Jallianwalla *Bagh* (Park) at a rally. These civilians were fired upon without warning under orders from General R.E.H. Dyer, who then proceeded to round up his troops and depart, leaving the dead, dying, and wounded at the scene. After the tragedy the entire Congress meeting in Amritsar rejected any talk of understanding between the British and India. Rabindranath Tagore returned the knighthood which had been conferred upon him after he won the Nobel Prize for Literature. The Indian people were overwhelmed with grief and horror and by the definite feeling that they wanted to be free of the British.

The growing Indian demands for self-rule had in the past

been countered by piecemeal statutes passed by the British, which gave the Indians a trickle of participation every so often. The chronology in Part Two details the various Indian Councils Acts, the Government of India Acts, as well as several other statutes through which the Indians gained slow and ineffective political participation. An advocate of this participation was Edwin Samuel Montagu, Secretary of State, who, along with Lord Chelmsford, had been working on the Montagu-Chelmsford Report of 1918, which then became the Government of India Act of 1919. The Act embodied the expansion of the electorate and a novel system of dual government called *Dyarchy* under which some aspects of administration would be *reserved* for the officers of the Crown and others *transferred* to Indians. However, after Jallianwalla Bagh, it was too little too late. The World War was over for Britain, but the confrontation with India had just begun.

Although there were some Indian national leaders who were willing to work within the reforms proposed by the Act of 1919, this changed in 1920 at Nagpur when Gandhi emerged as the man of the hour and then of the national movement, and he was not in the mood for niceties any longer. The Act of 1919 was not enough, said Gandhi. In 1920 he called for the first *satyagraha*, or truth struggle, against the British. Gandhi wanted everyone to practice non-cooperation with the British in every way possible so that the imperial machinery would be brought to a standstill. Believing vehemently that *every* Indian should be involved, Gandhi asked for mass support and unity among Indians of all backgrounds. Thus, hoping to win over even estranged members of the Muslim community, he accepted the Khilafat Movement *(See Part Two.)*

The response to Mahatma Gandhi was overwhelming. For the first time the masses from all walks of life in India, the rich, the poor, Hindus, Muslims, Sikhs, Christians, and eventually, the "untouchables" were involved in the national movement. It is a measure of the movement's strength that the 1921 visit of the Prince of Wales to India was boycotted to the embarrassment and fury of the British who reacted with even greater oppression afterwards.

As Mahatma Gandhi's appeal as a national leader grew by leaps and bounds across all communities and castes and languages, Jinnah and the Muslim League increasingly feared Hindu dominance and became convinced that the Muslims had to plan a separate future for themselves. In 1920 Jinnah left the Congress permanently, and by 1921 the tensions between the Hindu and Muslim communities escalated even further. As the issue of Hindu-Muslim separation became more and more articulated, it brought out the worst in all. The Hindu-Muslim problem, called communal violence in India, had come to stay, intermittently causing bloodshed while steadily spreading the poison of religious hatred in different parts of India.

Thus in spite of Gandhi's immense popularity, there was far too much tension and discord in the country, and his call for *satyagraha* erupted into violence, prompting him to call it off. He was jailed in 1922 after which he concentrated on social and economic issues for the next several years. In the absence of Gandhi, the Congress Party was then taken over by Motilal Nehru (father of Jawaharlal Nehru) and C.R. Das. These two leaders decided to participate in the 1923-24 elections (held under the Act of 1919) and work, even if it was in a limited way, within the governmental machinery.

In 1927 an all-white Indian Statutory Commission, called the Simon Commission, was appointed to evaluate Dyarchy and to formulate proposals for the next step in the process of giving Indians their own government. The Congress and the League boycotted this insulting deputation when it arrived in India in 1928, and the Commission was greeted everywhere with the admonishment to "go back." The Congress then took matters into its own hands and called an All-Parties Conference in order to draw up plans for a draft constitution under the supervision of Motilal Nehru. Jinnah objected to the status accorded to the Muslim electorate under the draft constitution, but his complaint was rejected by the Congress on the grounds that Jinnah did not speak for all Muslims.

Jinnah left the All-Parties Conference following the rejection of his complaint, and joined the All-India Muslim Conference under the leadership of the Aga Khan. The antagonism between Jinnah and the Congress became etched in stone. The All-India Muslim Conference passed a resolution demanding greater representation for the Muslims in the proposed central government. However, Jinnah was still dissatisfied with the lack of progress made by the Muslim leaders, as well as by their internal differences. In frustration he quit politics altogether in 1931 and lived in Britain for about five years.

In 1929 Lord Irwin had promised Indian leaders Dominion status. However, younger Congress members, such as Jawaharlal Nehru and Subhash Chandra Bose, now distrustful of the British and their political promises, would only accept *Purna Swarajya* (complete independence). They reflected well the sentiments of the entire nation which was now actively involved in the freedom movement. Another round of boycott and civil disobedience began in 1930 with Gandhi's salt march to Dandi. (*See Part Two.*) As a result of this march, thousands of members of the Indian National Congress (as well as Gandhi) were arrested.

There were some British efforts during this period to bring the main players on the Indian political scene together for discussions. Thus, the three Round Table Conferences were held between 1930 and 1932 in London. These three conferences did not succeed in bringing about any under-standing between the parties, and nothing was achieved in Britain. On the other hand, in India the national movement for independence continued to grow by the hour. The growing Congress demand for independence was accompanied by the growing movement among some Muslims for a separate na-tion which, as they envisaged it, would be created by the par-titioning of India. This movement was first given public ex-pression in 1930 when Sir Muhammed Iqbal, the poet, made the demand for a separate Muslim state.

The demand for separatism was satisfied to some extent in 1932 when the Communal Award was issued by the British Prime Minister, Sir Ramsey MacDonald. The Award granted separate electorates to Muslims, Sikhs, Christians, Anglo-In-dians, Europeans, and the Depressed Classes (which included the *untouchables)*. Needless to say, the Award did not meet with a good reception at the Congress camp since it was seen as a divisive measure aimed against Indian society, particu-larly the Hindus.

Gandhi, who had been unceremoniously imprisoned upon his return from the Second Round Table Conference in Lon-don, started a fast-unto-death in jail in protest against the Communal Award. He said that the untouchables were a part of the Hindu community, and the Award was calculated to "divide and rule" that community. While Gandhi was in Yeravada Prison, the leader of the untouchable community, Dr. B. R. Ambedkar, met with him for discussions, and the two concluded the revolutionary Yeravada Pact of 1932 which denounced untouchability. This event forced the British Government to eliminate separate electorates for the untouchables, and the Hindu community remained intact. For the first time in Indian history, in response to Gandhi's call, caste Hindus opened up temples and wells for the untouchables. Such was the charisma of Mahatma Gandhi that a centuries-old tradition was for the first time seriously questioned and condemned by the general population. However, the problem did not go away entirely, and Ambedkar was to spend the rest of his life fighting the injustice inherent in the deep-rooted caste system in Indian society.

In another slow step forward towards *eventual* self-rule for India, the Government of India Act was passed by the British Parliament in 1935. The Act provided for a federal government for India (which was never implemented), a Supreme Court, wider franchise, and separate electorates. Although the Act enlarged the participation of Indians in their government, it did not provide for self-rule, giving the ultimate authority to the Viceroy, and as such was another piecemeal concession to Indians. Though seen as divisive, the Act was accepted by the Congress as being better than nothing. Jinnah returned to India to ensure Muslim participation under the new constitution, and he subsequently became the chief catalyst for the revival of the Muslim League.

Elections under the new constitution established by the Government of India Act were held in 1936, and the Congress

Party won overwhelmingly in the elections. The lack of accommodation which Jinnah perceived on the part of the victorious Congress towards the Muslim League strengthened his conviction that the future of the Muslims of India could not be left in the hands of the Congress. Jinnah committed himself to a two-nation future for free India. Therefore, he embarked on a course which was ultimately to fulfill his dream of a separate Muslim nation, a dream which would complete the emotional and physical division of the subcontinent.

Because the Muslims were still divided among themselves, Jinnah realized that to achieve his aim he had to unite the various Muslim groups under the banner of the League. Earlier, the Muslim League movement had been elitist, but Jinnah succeeded within a short time span in bringing together a wide cross section of Muslims from all walks of life and geographical areas. Even at this stage not all Muslims joined the League, and tens of millions never joined it at all. These Indian Muslims dedicated themselves instead to fighting for India's independence from Britain. There were some renewed efforts made to bring the League and the Congress Party together, but neither side would have any part of it. Now there were three sides to the triangle: the British, the Congress, and the Muslim League.

The clouds of another world war were fast gathering even as the twin movements of liberation and separation continued to accelerate in India. In 1939 the reluctant honeymoon of the Congress Party and the British Raj was cut short by Lord Linlithgow's announcement of World War II. Lord Linlithgow told India that she was at war without so much as a "by-your-leave" to her leaders, who had begun to believe that they were going to play an intrinsic part in the government of their own country. The Congress Party resigned in protest. On the other hand, the Muslim League was grateful to be relieved of Congress Party rule. Jinnah passed a Thanksgiving Resolution on December 22, 1939, and asked the Muslims to observe that day as a Deliverance Day.

The Thanksgiving Resolution was followed by the Lahore Session of the Muslim League in 1940. At this session the Lahore Resolution was passed which stated that the unchangeable goal for Muslims was to establish a separate nation. Several proposals were put forward as to how this could be done, but the situation remained as deadlocked as before between the Congress and the League. Was it possible to avoid cutting up India into two parts? Meanwhile, the Congress Party went ahead with its agenda of independence for India and protest against the war effort. Law and order were frail commodities in India at the time, and violence was fast gaining the upper hand.

Soon World War II was in full swing, and Britain was immersed in the war. Japan was sweeping fast through Southeast Asia. This time India was not so forthcoming with help for her rulers for whom things looked precarious without Indian support. Hence, to assure Indians of the *bonafides* of the British Government, Prime Minister Attlee, with India experts, Cripps and Simon, submitted a plan for the formation of a Constituent Assembly for India which would draft a constitution for an independent India at the cessation of the war. In short, the Cripps Mission, sent to India in 1942, promised independence on condition of Indian support against Japan. Independence was now a done deal except for one problem: no one could decide *how* it was going to be done. If India were given complete independence, how would the demands of the

Muslim League and the Congress be reconciled? Meanwhile the Mission was rejected by the Congress Party because it allowed the provinces to opt out of the Mission Plan, and any kind of dismemberment of the nation was anathema to the party leaders. The mission also failed to commit itself to a full-fledged Indian Government. Thus, the deadlock over which way to go continued, and the Mission returned to Britain empty-handed.

Following the failure of the Cripps Mission, Mahatma Gandhi called for the British to *Quit India* in the interest of India's security which he felt was threatened by the Japanese who were on their way to India. (By May 1942, the Japanese were in Burma and pounding on the Assam-Burma border but were held off for two years.) For the first time a verbal injunction to the British to leave was expressed through the length and breadth of the country, and the nation rallied behind the Mahatma's cry. Mass arrests followed swiftly. This event came to be known as the "Quit India" Movement.

Jinnah and the Muslim League denounced the "Quit India" movement. This denunciation made it more than obvious to all concerned that the Congress Party and the League would always be on the opposite sides of *any* issue if the demands of the Muslim League were not met. At this rate Independence would remain a distant dream, and the country might suffer from spontaneous combustion before long.

The leaders of the freedom movement realized that the demand for Pakistan would *have* to be considered to resolve the crisis, and the Congress Party was persuaded to accept the idea of partition. The Congress asked C.R. Rajagopalachari, the eminent national leader and scholar, to devise a formula for a separate Muslim state. Gandhi met Jinnah to discuss

Rajagopalachari's formula, but again, no agreement could be reached between them as to the actual process of Partition.

World War II ended with the surrender of Germany in May and Japan in September 1945. The Labor Government in Britain sent a Cabinet Mission to India, headed by Lord Pethick Lawrence (and including the undaunted Sir Strafford Cripps), which arrived in India on March 24, 1946. The Cabinet Mission brought a plan in which the proposed governmental structure for free India was spelled out. The Congress and the League each found reasons to say that the proposal was unacceptable; thus again, nothing could be finalized. The Cabinet Mission returned to Britain without any of the details worked out and certainly without Jinnah's demand for a separate nation fulfilled.

After the failure of the Cabinet Mission, the disappointed Muslim League decided that it was time for Muslims to take matters into their own hands. Jinnah called for a Direct Action Day, a call which led to mayhem and murder throughout the country. Hindus and Muslims were torn apart as they had never been before. The ensuing chaos was but a whiff of the slaughter of 1947.

At the official level the constitutional process continued as Jawaharlal Nehru, at Viceroy Wavell's invitation, formed an Interim Government in 1946. The League reacted with public mourning and black flags. However, Liaquat Ali Khan and four other League members eventually joined the Interim Government.

An unsuccessful attempt was made by the British Government to bring Nehru, Jinnah, and Wavell to London to discuss a peaceful transfer of power to India. The fact was that in India there was already bloodshed and lawlessness everywhere and things did not look too promising. The British realized that they could not stay in India much longer and hurriedly packed their bags as best they could. As a result, without the logistics of partition having been worked out, Attlee announced in the House of Commons on February 20, 1947, that His Majesty's Government had resolved to transfer power to "responsible Indian hands" no later than June, 1948. The person chosen for the job was Lord Louis Mountbatten, who replaced Wavell.

Mountbatten called a meeting of Nehru, Jinnah, Sardar Vallabh Bhai Patel, Sardar Baldev Singh, and other Indian leaders. It was settled that India would be divided. The states with Congress Party majority would go to India; Sindh, Baluchistan, and the Northwest Frontier Province would go to the new state, and Bengal and Punjab would be divided between the two nations. The new Muslim state would soon be called Pakistan, or the Land of Purity, a name which had been chosen for it seventeen years before. East Bengal, while a part of the new state of Pakistan, was lodged in the eastern side of India, a subcontinent away from the rest of Pakistan. The plan was accepted by the invited leaders who represented all of the parties. It was then announced to the world that the date for transfer of power would be around the 15th of August, 1947.

On paper this conclusion to India's long quest for freedom looked tidy, but the deadly nightmare of partition was unfolding. Several steps had been taken to forestall the anticipated chaos, but as history was to show these were not enough. Thus, a Partition Committee was appointed to allocate assets between the two countries. Sir Cyril Radcliffe was asked to perform the impossible task of demarcating the frontier boundaries of the two nations; the demarcation was named the Radcliffe Award. Government officers and other public servants were given a choice as to which country they would serve. Even so, partition resulted in a very bloody birth for one country and a very bloody re-birth for the other. The migration of over ten million Hindus and Muslims in contrary directions to countries of their choice resulted in a massacre of about ten percent of the migrants. This brutality among erstwhile neighbors and friends has had a detrimental effect on the relationship between the two nations even to this day. It is important to point out that almost as many Muslims remained with India voluntarily as became part of Pakistan and that the Muslim population in India today is approximately the same as the entire population of Pakistan. The province of East Pakistan in Bengal, although Muslim, eventually rebelled against Pakistan and achieved independence in 1971 as Bangladesh ("land of the Bengali speaking peoples").

To complete the political re-organization of India, Mountbatten called a conference of the princes to determine where they would be aligned. When the dust had settled, most of the 600 princes, with the exception of the rulers of Hyderabad, Junagadh and Kashmir, joined India. Eventually, all three of these wavering princes also acceded to India under varying circumstances and conditions.

The Constituent Assembly became the Parliament of India; Jawaharlal Nehru became India's first Prime Minister; and Dr. Rajendra Prasad its first President. In Pakistan, Muhammed Ali Jinnah became Governor General of Pakistan, and Liaquat Ali Khan became the first Prime Minister.

CHAPTER SIX

How is India governed today?

India's government is a fascinating and important field of study because India represents some rather awesome numbers. The Indian nation contains a fifth of the world's total population, has the second largest population in the world, is the seventh largest nation in the world in area, and is the world's biggest functioning democracy. Thus, it is no surprise that Americans want to know more about India and her constitution and how this huge country is governed.

The constitution of the Republic of India (also called Bharat Varsha, Bharat, the Union of India, and the Indian Union) is the lengthiest written constitution in the world. It borrows features from the constitutions of several other nations, such as Great Britain, Ireland, the United States, and Canada. Like these countries, India places the greatest emphasis on the importance of each individual citizen, and this emphasis finds expression in the Fundamental Rights of Indian citizens, listed in the Constitution.

The year 1997 marks India's 50th year as a sovereign democratic republic. As a developing country, India has maintained a strong loyalty and commitment to the democratic process. Thus, in 1996 India conducted the world's largest elections as a result of which Indians once again replaced the party in power at the central government in a peaceful, democratic way. In fact, in the face of very limited resources, the Election Commission of India managed the world's largest electorate with remarkably few mishaps.

Elections in India are held under the supervision of the Chief Election Commissioner, who is a non-partisan officer.

The Indian electorate is based on the principle of Universal Adult Suffrage, and Indians turn out in vast numbers to cast their ballots. India's multi-party system provides the lifeblood for the democratic processes of the country. Over 52 percent of the electorate votes, which is a good indication of the fact that Indians are very involved in the process of the formation of their government.

The President of India is the constitutional or ceremonial head of state, whereas the real power lies with the head of the government, i.e., the Prime Minister of India. The President of India is the Commander-in-Chief of the Armed Forces (Army, Navy, and Air Force) which undertake the defense of the country, but each branch of the armed forces has its own Chief of Staff. The President is indirectly elected for five years by an electoral college composed of the two houses of Parliament and the state legislative assemblies.

The Vice President of India is indirectly elected by an electoral college composed of the two houses of Parliament. If the President dies in office, the Vice President becomes the President of India.

The executive branch of the Government of India is formed by the Prime Minister who is either the leader of the majority party or the leader of a coalition (combination) of parties commanding a majority in the legislature. The Prime Minister forms a Council of Ministers from elected members of his or her party, or his or her coalition. From the Council of Ministers the Prime Minister selects a Cabinet, and together with the President of India they constitute the executive branch of the government. In actual practice, under the constitution, powers are only symbolically held by the President and are actually exercised by the Prime Minister of India and the Council of Ministers.

The Prime Minister is the real chief executive, but this power is kept in check by the legislature. The legislative branch of government in India is the Parliament, which is a bicameral (two chambered) legislature. The Parliament is composed of the directly elected *Lok Sabha* (House of the People) and the indirectly elected *Rajya Sabha* (Council of States). The *Lok Sabha* is composed of not more than 550 representatives and the *Rajya Sabha* is composed of not more than 250 members. The *Rajya Sabha* has far fewer powers than the *Lok Sabha*.

The Prime Minister and the Council of Ministers are answerable to the Parliament. If the government loses its majority in the *Lok Sabha*, it must resign. Thus, India is in actual practice a parliamentary democracy very much like that of Great Britain.

The judiciary in India is composed of the Supreme Court at the center, the High Courts and district and local courts in the states. The Supreme Court of India, which heads the judicial system, is formed by a Chief Justice and not more than seventeen judges, who are appointed by the President of India. The independence of the judiciary is ensured by their method of appointment and removal which is delineated in the constitution.

Although there is a separation of powers between the executive, legislative, and judicial branches, this separation is not watertight. The three branches of government keep an eye on each other through a system of checks and balances just as they do in the United States.

The federal republic of India consists of twenty-five states and seven Union Territories (which do not have the full powers of states). The states are: Andhra Pradesh, Arunachal

Pradesh, Assam, Bihar, Goa, Gujarat, Haryana, Himachal Pradesh, Jammu and Kashmir, Karanataka, Kerala, Madhya Pradesh, Maharashtra, Manipur, Meghalaya, Mizoram, Nagaland, Orissa, Punjab, Rajasthan, Sikkim, Tamil Nadu, Tripura, Uttar Pradesh, and West Bengal. The Union Territories are: Andaman and Nicobar Islands, Chandigarh, Dadra and Nagar Haveli, Daman and Diu, Delhi, Lakshadweep, and Pondicherry. The governmental structure in the states closely resembles the structure of the central government.

India is a federation with a strong bias towards the central government. The national government deals with issues of national concern, such as defense, foreign affairs, currency, and post and telegraph. The state governments handle those issues which are primarily regional in character, such as public health, education, and local government. It is fair to say, however, that that the overriding powers in India lie with the central government. Thus it is often stated that India is a *federation* with very strong *unitary* features.

CHAPTER SEVEN

What lifestyles exist in India?

India today has two distinct lifestyles, rural and urban, and both are very different from each other. Most of India is agricultural, and most Indians are poor by international standards. On the other hand, India contains some of the oldest living cultural centers in the world, and some of its newer cities are extremely cosmopolitan and wealthy.

Since most of India is rural, we'll take a look at the villages first. It would not be an exaggeration to say that village life in India has not changed much over the centuries except for electricity and some modern transportation and communication. In general, villages have only a few brick houses, and most villagers live in mud houses thatched with straw, a building style which has been followed for centuries. Modern architects have also found that this is generally the best type of housing for villages. The huts make optimal use of locally available materials and are well suited to the habitat in terms of the weather, which can sometimes be very hot, humid, and wet.

Electricity is not as dependable in India as it is here in the United States, but hardly any village is without it. Unfortunately, overwhelming demand has resulted in frequent shortages and equipment breakdowns, making the inadequacy of the present output quite apparent. However, this problem is being addressed seriously, and the energy sector is in the process of being brought up-to-date. *(See Chapter Thirteen.)*

The most commonly-used vehicle in the villages are bullock carts with bicycles coming in a close second. Buses and trains connect villages to each other and to the cities. People in the rural areas lead very simple lives with few modern residential amenities or electrical gadgets. Indian villagers work very hard in what are often very difficult climatic conditions with very few comforts. Most villagers do not have telephones, televisions, or any modern conveniences as such. However, villages are connected by government-owned telephone, post and telegraph services. The government-owned facilities sometimes possess the only television set in the village as well. This situation is beginning to change, and rural India is becoming more prosperous and up-to-date each year. (*See Chapter Thirteen.*)

The prosperity of rural India is due mainly to the progress made in Indian agriculture, which seems to have finally shaken off its stupor as increased agricultural productivity has led to a spurt in the economic life of the villages. There is a night and day difference between food availability just after independence in 1947 and today. In fact, India now exports food grains to other countries after she feeds her own people. Even so, rural India still has a long way to go before her masses can enjoy relatively comfortable and modern lifestyles.

Although most of India is in her villages, urban areas exist all over the country and are home to millions of Indians. Cities in India are like urban areas in any major developing country. There are many brick and stone houses in towns, and plenty of multi-storied buildings in the cities. Through ancient times travelers have noted the multistoried houses they saw in India so this is nothing new!

The largest group of people in the cities belong to the middle class, which is composed of government employees, engineers, doctors, lawyers, businessmen, academics, artists, journalists, corporate executives, etc. The Indian middle class alone is equal in number to the entire population of the United States of America. This group has large disposable incomes and enjoys all the advantages of modern technology. They drive cars or ride motor scooters, and their houses and apartments are fitted with television sets, refrigerators, and air-conditioning. All of these items are made in India under many Indian brand names.

To meet the needs generated by such a large number of office-going commuters, buses and trains are available in the cities. In general, though, Indian public transportation is vastly inadequate and cannot meet the pressure created by the population growth. The traffic in the cities is very heavy at all times; the roads are crowded; and the problem is exacerbated by the rapid acquisition of private automobiles by urban Indians.

The proliferation of privately-owned cars is just one clue to the fact that Indians love to live well and spend vast amounts of money on all kinds of household equipment, clothing, and entertainment. An abundance of paying consumers in the cities and in some villages has created a seemingly insatiable market for consumer durables and non-durables. Retailers cannot stock items for long, and their customers are generally waiting for the next shipment. Companies making consumer goods such as soaps and shampoos even take their advertisements to the villages now, creating demand for new toiletry goods among folks who have used the same cosmetics for thousands of years!

Lifestyles in India vary according to the income level of a person, as well as his or her residential location. The rural areas are generally quite backward in terms of amenities compared to the cities. The cities are better off in the sense that they have modern amenities and a higher standard of living. However, they cannot be immune to the economic conditions of rural India, as a result of which cities are besieged by the influx of job-hungry villagers. The pressures created by the constant arrival of millions from the rural areas naturally take their toll on the infrastructure in the urban areas. The industrial areas in particular attract large numbers of villagers who come in search of employment

In conclusion, one could say that there is a broad spectrum of lifestyles in India. The rich are very rich; the poor, most of whom are extremely poor, form the largest segment of society; and in between the two extremes lies a huge and prosperous middle class.

CHAPTER EIGHT

What is Indian apparel?

The traditional dress for most Indian women is the *sari*, a length of fabric, usually six yards long, which is draped around the body and worn over a blouse and underskirt. The sari may be worn in its classical form as well as in regional variations. In the north, the women also wear a *lehnga* (voluminous skirt), a *choli* (small blouse), and an *odhni* (very large, long scarf). Another outfit worn by women in the north is a *kameez* (long shirt) with a *salwar* (baggy pant) and a *dupatta* (another type of large, long scarf). In the winter women wear shawls, particularly in the north.

Men's traditional dress also differs according to various regions in India. However, except in cold climates, men all over India wear a length of fabric around their waist and a shirt on top. In the north men also wear loose pants called *pajamas*, and yes, that is where we get the word "pajama." *Pajama* literally means a dress for the legs.

Some tribal areas of India have very colorful dresses, which are different from the main Indian dress forms. The members of these tribes also wear, as a matter of course, several adornments made of beads, shells, bone, feathers, etc.

In Kashmir both women and men wear the famous Kashmir shawl. The Kashmiris have been weaving these warm shawls to protect themselves from the frigid Himalayan winters for countless generations. Therefore, it is not surprising that the beauty and warmth of these shawls have been mentioned in historical references from over two thousand years ago. One type of shawl is called *shah tus*. Made from the softest Himalayan goat hairs, *shah tus* is so gossamer-like that an entire shawl of several yards can pass through a ring. When the Scottish mills replicated this soft wool, they called it cashmere, and now you know why.

Centuries ago (during the reign of Zainulabidin in the 15th century according to some sources) Kashmir also introduced the world to intricate tapestry shawls called *Jamavar,* which were very much sought after in Europe. According to hearsay, Napolean's Josephine was a great collector of these splendid fabrics. When mills in Paisley, Scotland, started to manufacture imitations of *Jamavar* patterns in the early years of the nineteenth century, the shawl industry in Kashmir collapsed and was almost dead by 1870. Fortunately, government support and tremendous national patronage have given the Kashmir shawl industry a glorious revival today.

Formal or festive attire for Indians is basically the same style of clothing that is worn everyday except that it is made in more elaborate fabrics. Saris of silk and gold have been woven in ancient cities, like Kanchipuram and Varanasi, for centuries, and that is where women go even today to pick the finest fabrics. In addition, women wear fine jewelry for special occasions. The men in formal attire might wear jackets, scarves with gold borders around the neck, or an elaborate shawl. They also may wear waistcoats, turbans, or hats. However, turbans are worn everyday by most members of the Sikh community. All dress items differ from region to region, as do their names.

Today, traditional Indian dress is worn by a majority of

the people although Western dress is the norm for office-going men. Interestingly, women almost always wear Indian dresses to work. However, in keeping with the requirements of modern life, the fabrics traditionally used for clothing, i.e., cotton and silk, are quickly being replaced by easily-laundered synthetic fibers.

❧ CHAPTER NINE ❧

What is Indian cuisine?

Indian cuisine differs from area to area. For example, rice and wheat are the staples in areas where each grows easily; seafood is traditional in the coastal areas; and dried vegetables and dehydrated fish are customary foods in areas with very harsh winters. One look at a map of India will show the different climates and terrain of this geographically diverse country. These geographical variations create tremendous diversity in regional cuisine. *(See Chapter Three.)*

Almost everyone is aware that vegetarianism is very popular in India. The popularity of vegetarianism is probably due to the fact that hot weather in most of the country reduces the importance of meat in a diet. The other more certain reason for the large number of vegetarians in India is the prevailing ethos of non-violence in Jainism and Buddhism, which has had a great impact on animal slaughter in India. In any case, vegetarian cuisine is safer to eat in the absence of refrigeration, a luxury which most people in India do not enjoy.

Indian cuisine is well-known for its use of spices and herbs. Some of the spices and herbs grown in India are cardamon, cumin, turmeric, saffron, cinnamon, peppercorns, and nutmeg, to mention a few. Not surprisingly, some of these spices are used by Indians even for everyday meals.

An everyday Indian meal includes bread (leavened and unleavened) or rice and either a stew of vegetables and/or meat (commonly called curry) or a lentil soup called *dal*. This basic meal is garnished with some salad, pickle, and yogurt. Naturally, the number of dishes depends upon the economic background of the family. In any case, yogurt and pickles are almost mandatory and are sometimes the only accompaniment to rice or bread. Desserts are usually reserved for festive occasions and are made mostly of milk solids, *ghee* (clarified butter), and sugar.

This is as good a place as any to mention that India grows a great variety of rice grains, the most elegant of which is *Basmati*, or Queen of Fragrance, which I mention because it seems to have taken the United States by storm. In fact, Texas grows its own now, to the delight of all *Basmati* fans in America.

If you travel through north India, you will find that no matter how hot the weather gets, tea is served everywhere. Indians, in my opinion, are the world's greatest tea drinkers and would consume it all day, if possible. Curious tourists in India are told that hot tea is the most cooling drink.

In view of the popularity of the beverage, the history of tea in India requires some attention. China is the birthplace of tea as a beverage, from there it spread to other areas in the last decade of the 6th Century. However, from 1600 to 1858 it was the British East India Company which controlled the worldwide trade in tea. Every student of U. S. history knows that the colonists were some of the most avid tea drinkers and that the world's greatest tea party in Boston in 1773 eventually led to the American Revolution.

Tea led to some interesting events in the East as well. In order to bring the "cup that cheers" to the world as it were, the British encouraged tea cultivation in the temperate hills of east and south India, and soon India replaced China as the world's biggest tea exporter. *(See Part Two.)* There are now many varieties of tea in India i.e., Assam, Nilgiri, and Darjeeling, of which the world knows Darjeeling tea the best.

As tea is the staple in the north, so is coffee the staple in the south of India where it is consumed with equal vigor and frequency. In fact, coffee was also introduced by the British in the Nilgiri Hills in the south and did quite well for a while. However, after disease ravaged coffee crops, tea became the crop of choice in the beverage sector. Coffee is grown only in south India today, largely for domestic tastes and consumption. South Indian coffee is rich and delicious and has now become popular all over India.

CHAPTER TEN

What about leisure time?

What do Indians do in their spare time? How do they relax? Well, while family celebrations and gatherings take up the lion's share of spare time in India, there are several other leisure-time activities as well.

The most popular form of entertainment in the country is going to the cinema. Indians love the movies. Admission is fairly inexpensive, and Indian movie idols are so popular that when they run for any office, they are voted in by overwhelming majorities! India produces almost a thousand movies a year, the highest number of movies produced by any single country. Most of these are fantasy or "escape" musical films made for popular appeal. Notable exceptions to this rule are the movies of Satyajit Ray, who was one of the greatest film directors in the world. Ray created poignantly Indian film classics which continue to be exhibited and admired in India and around the world. In recognition of his contribution to the film industry, he received the most prestigious international film awards and was awarded a special "Oscar" shortly before his death in India.

Radio and television have also become integral parts of Indian life today. Until very recently, television operated under a government monopoly, and the repertoire of offerings was limited. Now commercial channels are allowed, and are fast multiplying through the facilities of satellite television. This has interesting cultural side effects in a country where some people who are still living ancient lifestyles are suddenly confronted with the technology and bizarre revelations of modern cable television from around the world. One can only speculate if this is entirely beneficial to a culture that is five thousand years old.

The next popular diversion in India certainly has to be indoor and outdoor sports. When talking about indoor sports, one must begin with chess, India's classical game. As the sport of India's kings, chess has in the past played a part in her literature, in her architecture (where the entire courtyard of a monarch might be designed as a chess board with live pawns moving at the monarch's command), and in many other situations as well. On a more everyday note, chess is one of the most popular indoor sports among old and young alike in India today. Parcheesi (or Ludo) also has its origins in India, and there is a theory that playing cards originated in India as well. Both games enjoy tremendous popularity in India.

Among traditional outdoor Indian sports are *kabaddi* and *guli danda*. In *kabaddi* each team sends out a challenger who has to take a deep breath, go across to the other side, touch an opponent, and return uncaught while still holding his breath. In *guli danda*, the players (who can vary in number) play with a *guli* (a wooden puck shaped like a miniature football) and a *danda* (a wooden stick). The puck must be hit in such a way that it flips over, is hit again, and flies. The winner is the one whose *guli* flies the farthest. Not all outdoor sports in India have ancient Indian origins. Cricket, a gift of the British, is probably the most popular outdoor sport in India, and the international test matches bring the country to a virtual standstill. Some of the other popular outdoor sports are field hockey, soccer (called football in India), and wrestling.

On a more sedentary note, Indians love to read and are

very news-hungry folks. The fact that hundreds of languages are spoken in the country has resulted in India's extraordinary publication of almost 4,000 daily newspapers, most of which are in local languages. There are excellent national English daily newspapers as well. In fact, India boasts the largest number of English dailies and periodicals in the world. India also annually publishes many books and over 600 scientific periodicals.

Indians also enjoy classical, folk, and popular music tremendously. India has a wealth of classical music which is centuries-old and has been widely patronized by its royalty. There are two main styles of classical music in India: North Indian or *Hindustani* and South Indian or *Carnatic* (the term is derived from the word *Karnataka,* but does not refer solely to that region). There are hundreds of *Ragas* (musical compositions) and many schools of classical vocal and instrumental music. It may interest the reader to know that the word Reggae comes from the Sanskrit word *Raga.* The most popular instruments in India are string instruments such as the *sitar* (made popular in the West by Ravi Shankar and the Beatles), the *veena*, the *sarangi,* the *sarod,* and the *santoor;* drums such as the *tabla* and the *mridangam*; and wind instruments such as the *shehnai,* the flute, and the *nagaswaram,* among others.

If India loves music so much, can dance be far behind? Not at all, for dance is beloved both in its classical and popular forms. There are five main schools of Indian classical dance, and they come from different parts of the country.

The most well-known school of dance is the *Bharatya Natyam* which is from Tamil Nadu. This dance is based on the *Natya Shastra,* an ancient treatise on the art of theater written by Bharata in the early centuries of the Christian era. In India theater was developed as part of worship, and until the early decades of the twentieth century the *Bharata Natyam* could only be performed as a temple dance, never publicly. (The next-door state of Andhra Pradesh has given birth to the *Kuchipudi* style which is based on the *Bharata Natyam*, but which has developed distinctive elements in its native state.) From the state of Kerala comes the ancient *Kathakali* dance in which the dancers (traditionally male only) represent mythological characters from the Hindu epics in exaggerated make-up and gestures. The north's contribution to classical dance is the *Kathak*, a formal dance in which complex rhythms are beautifully executed. The *Kathak* was developed within the protocol of the Muslim courts of north India. It is believed to be an ancestor of the flamenco dance of Spain where it is said to have arrived via the gypsies who went to Europe from Asia. From the eastern state of Manipur comes the *Manipuri,* a dance distinguished by the doll-like beautiful garments of the women dancers, as well as its mythological themes and devotional music. The state of Orissa is the birth-place of the *Orissi,* a dance also based on the *Natya Shastra*, which has been performed from antiquity. The themes of the *Orissi* are set to love songs, and when the dancers perform, they seem to reflect the lyrical steps of the sculptured dancers found in the ancient temples from that region.

On a popular level, Indians go to see folk dance and folk theater in the villages during cultural and religious *melas,* or village fairs. Puppet and shadow plays and folk musicians are among the most popular events. *Melas* are an important and regular feature of village life and have kept the tradition of handicrafts and folk arts alive in India. Now the popularity of these rural traditions has spread to metropolitan cities as well.

Finally, mention must be made of *mushairas* and *sammelans* (poetical soirees). These soirees, along with musical gatherings, continue a traditional pastime known for ages. Some marathon musical events last for a few days without a break, even at night! These events were among my favorite entertainments when I lived in India. Young and old alike stayed up until dawn, helped along by cups of delicious hot tea. At Kashmiri weddings, a nightlong music and dance performance held in honor of the bride or groom, is concluded by a stirring song called *Gulrez,* which slowly accompanies the rising sun until morning arrives in all its glory.

❧ CHAPTER ELEVEN ❧

What religions? What festivals?

The constitution of India is secular, which means that it is not based on any religion. However, religion has played a very important part in the history of the subcontinent for many centuries and continues to do so even today. Religion is a very powerful factor not only in the personal lives of most Indians, but in their social and political lives as well. In fact, India has been preoccupied with religion and its philosophy for millennia. This should not come as a surprise since India is the birthplace of four faiths: Hinduism; Sikhism; Buddhism; and Jainism.

Hindus constitute the largest religious group in India and number well over 800 million. Hinduism is the oldest living religion in the world, the earliest glimpse of which can, according to some, be seen in the Indus Valley Civilization. The next and definitive stage in the evolution of Hinduism took place in the early centuries after the advent of the Aryans in the north of India. During this period the Aryans developed the Vedas, the underlying texts of Hinduism. However, even at this stage the religion can only be identified properly as Vedism. It was the eventual absorption of innumerable indigenous tribal beliefs, deities, and symbols (already in place in India) into the Vedic pantheon, as well as the propounding of subsequent philosophies, which created the huge corpus of beliefs which we know today as Hinduism. How did this religion get its name? The people living near the Sindh River had been named *Hindus* by the Persians over two thousand years ago, and as we know, the name stuck! Later, the beliefs and way of life of the *Hindus* came to be called the *Hindu* faith by the Arabs who arrived in the subcontinent in the latter half of the first millennium A.D. Much later the English would call these beliefs *Hinduism,* a term which is now used by everyone, even by English-speaking Hindus. Traditionally, Hinduism is referred to as *Sanatan Dharma.*

Unlike many other religions, Hinduism, which developed over thousands of years, does not have one authoritative scripture or source. However, it is fair to say that the critical treatises of Hinduism are the Vedas, the oldest of which is the Rg Veda, upon which the other Vedas are based. Many other texts are also intrinsic to Hinduism, and are based on, or connected to, the Vedas, although they were compiled later. The earliest Hindu texts are classified as *Shruti* (or revealed), and the later texts are classified as *Smriti (*or remembered). It is outside my expertise to go into the details of these texts or philosophies, but I hope that the following will serve to give you a gist of this religion which has been evolving for 3500 years. Happily, there is no dearth of wonderful books on this subject for the reader who is interested in pursuing this field.

The language of most Hindu texts is Sanskrit, and the most prominent of these texts are the Vedas, followed by the Epics, and other texts.

The Vedas, also called Samhitas (collections)

1. *Rg Veda*   Verses or hymns

2. *Sama Veda*   Melodic arrangements for the hymns

3. *Yajur Veda*   Sacrificial chants

4. *Atharva Veda* Magical chants

Each Veda is composed of the following parts:

1. *Mantra*   Verse or hymn
2. *Brahmana*   Ritual prayer explanations and chants for the priest
3. *Upanishad*   Discussions resulting from philosophers' gatherings
4. *Aranyaka*   Collection of textbooks for hermits or forest dwellers

Epics

1. *Mahabharata*

2. *Ramayana*

The *Mahabharata* and the *Ramayana* are the major epics of Hinduism, sacrosanct stories which enjoy unrivaled popularity and authority among Hindus to this day. Both simplify and express Hindu philosophy through the lifestories of the epic heroes, the Pandava brothers and Rama, respectively. There are several other exemplary figures in the Epics, far too numerous to list here. (Naturally, the stories also include characters one must not emulate!) The *Ramayana* and the *Mahabharata* have been used as handbooks or guidelines for a proper Hindu life by the common man through the centuries.

The Epics are also the richest source of mythology in India. The figures from Hindu mythology are colorful and fascinating and exude a classic charm as they fly around on their *vahanas* (flying machines), slay demons, fall in love, conspire to make mischief, and endure epic trials and tribulations. It is perhaps no wonder, then, that Hindu mythological figures continue, even at the dawn of the twenty-first century, to enjoy the undying devotion of fans of all ages. Today Indians of all religious backgrounds raptly watch the ancient antics and accomplishments of these mythological figures as they are serialized on television.

The *Mahabharata*, generally considered to be compiled by the great sage Veda Vyasa, is about eight times the length of *The Iliad* and *The Odyssey* combined and, not surprisingly, has the distinction of being the longest book in the world. The *Mahabharata* is the saga of the five righteous Pandava brothers and their struggle against their not-so-righteous cousins, the Kaurava brothers. This conflict results in a cataclysmic battle. The *Mahabharata* includes the *Bhagavad Gita*, or *Song of the Lord,* the longest philosophical poem in the world. Called the *Gita,* this poem is a discussion between two righteous protagonists, Lord Krishna and Arjuna, about the guiding principles of a Hindu life, and it is one of the most revered and sacred texts in Hinduism. The *Gita* is used today by Hindus as a working Bible for the swearing-in procedure in India where a very British court system is alive and well.

Valmiki, another legendary sage, is considered to be the author of the *Ramayana*, which deals with the life of the hero-king Rama and with his accession to the throne at Ayodhya. The actual events of the Epics, which form the germ around which cocoon-like accretions have developed through the years, took place much earlier than the first-recorded compilation. The *Ramayana* was completed later than the *Mahabharata* although there is some controversy about which came first. The probable period for some events in both Epics is estimated to be the early centuries of the millennium before the Christian era.

Other Texts

Hinduism and Hindu philosophy continued to evolve with the passage of time, passing from generation to generation. Needless to say, everything that was handed down was not obeyed and followed unquestioningly for centuries. Discussions and considerations among philosophers gave birth to new philosophies. Among these are the Six Schools or Systems of Indian Philosophy. These schools or systems are the Nyaya; Vaisheshika; Sankhya; Yoga; Purva Mimansa; and the Vedanta. The literature of these schools of thought is a vast and endless source of philosophical work, far beyond this book and author, both in content and quantity.

As can be imagined, for a Hindu eager to master his or her spiritual heritage, the physical task of reading these vast literary tracts is daunting enough, not to mention memorizing them or comprehending their phenomenal philosophic content. In ancient times human ingenuity came to the rescue of aspiring Hindus in the form of *Sutras*, or synopses, which are encapsulated explanations of important texts or doctrines. The *sutra* (or thread) was designed as a guideline for a person to hold in order to recall the entire text. Thus the *Dharma Sutras* were synopses of Hindu texts on Dharma or law. The *Dharmashastras* (or theories and laws of social and ethical life) were based on the Dharma Sutras.

The earliest *Dharmashastra* is the *Manu Smriti*, or Code of Manu, which is dated from the earliest centuries of the Christian Era. Considered by many Hindus to be the lawbook for the correct Hindu life, *Manu Smriti* encodes the ritualistic obligations and conduct upon which Hindu society eventually patterned itself. Although Manu is a mythological figure and a legendary author, his code is regarded by orthodox

Hindus as the most important *Dharmashastra*. The Code of Manu is followed to some extent even today; understandably, after two thousand years, parts of this guide need to be over-hauled and updated.

The oldest historical texts in India are the *Puranas* (loosely translated, the Ancients) which are also a rich source of mythology. First compiled in the Gupta Era, these texts narrate legends tracing genealogies and events from virtually prehistoric times. The *Puranas* were compiled much later than the earliest events they detail, but they tally with some known events when they describe later periods.

This broad outline indicates the breadth of the ocean of texts intrinsic to Hinduism. The importance of these texts is obvious from the generally held belief that a Hindu receives spiritual merit by the recitation of any of these texts or even by *listening* to these recitations. The fact remains that for most Hindus a major part of their spiritual literature remains unread. For example, as much as I would have loved to read these texts from cover to cover, my ignorance of Sanskrit prevents me from doing so (although there are translations of some of these texts in place now). This problem is compounded by the fact that there is *so much* to read and comprehend. As a Hindu, however, one hears *slokas,* or verses, from the Vedas recited at important moments in one's life and manages to memorize some of them. I have tried to present the few verses I know to my daughters at important milestones in their lives such as their yearbook dedications when they graduated from high school or college.

Even though most Hindus are not well-versed in their re-ligious books, this has not precluded them from being obser-vant or devout. If you ask most Hindus what makes them a

Hindu, the answer is likely to be that they were born a Hindu. The fact is that in the absence of any *one* particular text and in the presence of a *multitude* of explanations, Hinduism is a way of life that a person follows based upon individual family observances. There is no single organizational hierarchy or church which all or a major group of Hindus accept to the exclusion of others, and deities enjoy importance more on the basis of local popularity than on the basis of any one universally accepted rule. There are, however, some essential features in which all Hindus by and large believe, at least in part. A rough list of these features, a list by no means indisputable, is as follows:

1. **The four castes**: *Brahmin* (the priestly class); *Kshatriya* (the warrior class); *Vaishya* (the merchant class); and *Shudra* (the low or menial caste).
2. **The four *ashrams*, or stages, of a person's life**: *Brahmacharya* (bachelor—studenthood); *Grihastha* (family life); *Vanaprastha* (meditative life); and *Sanyas* (renunciation of material life).
3. ***Purushartha,* or the four values by which one must live**: *Dharma* (the Law of righteous life); *Artha* (material well-being); *Kama* (desire for the enjoyment of life); and *Moksha* (liberation from the cycles of re-birth).
4. The belief in **Brahman** (or *Paramatma,* the Supreme *Atma,* Consciousness, Soul, or God) and the belief in man as part of this *Brahman*.
5. The belief in **Samsara** or the rebirth or reincarnation of man and the transmigration of the soul after death to another living being.
6. The belief in **Moksha**, or liberation from the cycles of

rebirth by actions, knowledge, and devotion. *Moksha* can be achieved by several ways:

a. Righteous living and righteous acts, according to the laws of *Dharma* and *Karma;*
b. Belief in the trinity of *Brahma* (the Creator of the Universe), *Vishnu* (the Preserver), and *Siva* (the Destroyer);
c. Belief in *Shakti,* or the female or creative half of the cosmos, in any or all of her forms such as *Durga, Bhawani,* and *Kali* (to name a few forms);
d. Belief in *Bhakti,* or personal devotion to a particular deity.

This is a broad outline of major Hindu beliefs, and by no means does it cover every belief prevalent in India.

A question I am asked very often is how such a philosophical religion as Hinduism can have such primitive beliefs as animal and plant worship. A simple answer is that since Hinduism is the oldest continuous living religion, some forms of worship common to all ancient religions have persisted in Hinduism. Among these forms of worship, which ancestors of mankind all over the world once observed, is the worship of nature in its animal, tree, or other forms.

Hinduism, as old as it is, continues to grow in numbers and continues to travel abroad as it did centuries ago. It is no stranger to the United States of America now, and many temples have been constructed to minister to the large Hindu population here. Some words from Hinduism are now familiar to Americans too. For example, there is much talk about *karma, mantra,* and *nirvana.* Most people in the United States are familiar with the word *yoga* since the physical exercises which are a part of the *Hatha Yoga* school have become very popular all over the world. *Hatha Yoga* has also found favor with many Western doctors who recommend some of its meditation exercises as a way to lowering blood pressure and treating other ailments as well. Actually, a person who practices yoga, as envisaged in the strict sense of the term, disciplines himself in *every* way. The physical exercises are only one part of the system, the ultimate aim of which is to be prepared in body and spirit to attain salvation.

The unbroken history of Hinduism means that the religion retains many aspects, some desirable and some not, which are thousands of years old. Among the less desirable traditions retained by Hinduism has been the perpetuation of a rigid caste system.

Regarded as an intrinsic part of the Hindu religion, the caste system originated in occupational divisions (i.e. priests, warriors, merchants, and lower or menial castes). In earlier times, although the distinction between the castes was fairly clear-cut, there was vertical and horizontal mobility among the castes. However, with the passage of time, the system became rigidified and fossilized to the point that a person's social status was determined once and for all by the caste of his parents. Thus, society was classified by caste-at-birth. At the lower end, stratification resulted in the oppressively inhuman practice of "untouchability" where the untouchables were treated like pariahs and contaminated beings. Thanks to the charisma and leadership of Mahatma Gandhi, this practice was dealt a fatal blow in the early twentieth century, for under his leadership untouchability was for the first time denounced through the length and breadth of the country. *(See Part Two.)* Post-independence legislation has also brought

India into the twentieth century on these and other socio-religious issues.

Hindus today no longer adhere to the traditional occupation of their birth castes so in a sense mobility has returned. For example, I come from a Brahmin, or priestly, caste, but a fair number of my relatives are soldiers and businessmen, and none of them are priests.

Most modern Indians do not pay heed to the caste system and its traditions. However, the fact remains that even if one does not believe in the caste system, those who *do* believe in it will *know* what caste one belongs to because it is inherent in one's family name. In short, one's caste is unchangeable not because one is not worthy of or is superior to another caste, but because one's caste at birth is inherent in the family name as a kinship symbol. A family name can be changed, but then it would no longer be a family name, carrying lineage and kinship.

The kinship marker of caste is so rooted in the Vedic times and so intrinsic to the subcontinent that it is not something only the Hindus follow. Even Pakistan, which is an Islamic state, but which has had a common cultural heritage with India, has castes entered in land records as a way of determining lineage. Similarly, there are castes even among the Sikhs who specifically discarded casteism in their religion.

Today there are some ramifications of the caste system that could not have been dreamed of in Vedic times. In the national elections in India this year, caste has proven to be of great political importance for certain disadvantaged groups as they gathered under an umbrella of kinship and voting muscle which helped them to overthrow the party in power.

Caste has also provided electoral support for other politicians in India in the past, but never in such large measure.

In appreciation of the history of injustice resultant from the caste system, certain provisions (such as reservations and quotas) have been made in the Indian constitution and under the laws of India, which are intended to bring everyone in society up to par. Needless to say, this is not always easy and comes with its own set of imponderables, but there can be no doubt that by and large these proactive steps have worked. Today members of what was formerly the "untouchable" caste are well-represented in all walks of life. A person's place in Indian society today is based on his or her occupation and achievement, rather than caste, and it is not uncommon to find a person of a so-called higher caste working as a subordinate of a person who comes from a so-called lower caste. This would have been unthinkable just 50 years ago.

In spite of today's reforms, the caste system has without question kept some sections of Indian society woefully deprived of social status, benefits, and progress. Under India's constitution, discrimination for any reason is not allowed, and one can only imagine (and hope) that with the spread of technology and education, the last vestiges of the millennia-old baggage of caste will disappear. However, when a civilization is thousands of years old, fifty years is too short a time to make a *complete* change. Discrimination based on the caste system still prevails in parts of India, even if it is illegal and unconstitutional.

Two other questions I am often asked about Indians are, "Do you *really* have arranged marriages?" and "Why do you wear a "dot" on your forehead?" The answer to the first question is YES. In India, just as in the world over until very recently, people do have arranged marriages. This is not prescribed by religion, but rather is a matter of convenience and tradition in a society where dating is confined only to a microscopic minority in the metropolitan cities. This does not mean that love itself is not prevalent in India! The literature of India, her prose and poetry, her folk songs and dances, and her paintings, abound in love themes of all types, some proper and some not quite. However, the general opinion seems to be that marriage is too important and lifelong (sometimes through many lives) a decision and that dating has nothing to do with it.

As far as the intriguing "dot," variously called a *bindi*, a *tikka*, or a *namam*, (and several other names in different parts of India) is concerned, there are many answers to that one. One answer is that according to Hindu tradition, the forehead is the seat of the highest spiritual power in the body, and the "dot" symbolizes that power. Then again, some Indians think they look better with color on their forehead! Also, people sometimes get the "dot" on their foreheads as part of a religious service, rather like ashes on the foreheads of Catholics at Lent. In any event, the "dot" is not mandatory, but is a matter of individual choice and tradition.

The preservation of ancient traditions in Hinduism owes much to the Brahmins. This powerful priestly class exercised unquestioned authority because of their virtual monopoly over the knowledge of the religious literature of the Hindus, their ability to read and write Sanskrit, their ability to perform sacrifices (an integral aspect of the Aryan culture), and their ability to recite the chants which accompanied the *yagna* (sacrifices). Their chants were usually part of a command per-

formance for a monarch or chieftain. The common man naturally felt left out and looked elsewhere for his personal spiritual solace. This search gave birth to Buddhism and Jainism
in the sixth century B.C. Both religions rejected prevalent
Brahministic Hinduism as the final word and dwelt more on
the individual as the means to his own salvation. In fact the
first powerful challenge to Hinduism and to the Brahmins
who had shaped it, came from Buddhism and Jainism, followed two millenia later by the fourth religion born in India,
i.e., Sikhism. I shall endeavor to give the reader a basic idea of
the tenets of these three religions in the following pages.

The founder of the Buddhist religion was Gautama Buddha, who, as Prince Siddhartha, was agonized by the human
misery he saw about him. When still a young prince, Siddhartha renounced his kingdom, his family, and all his material possessions because he felt that the world was full of
pain and suffering. He retreated to the forests to find the way
to avoid all pain and to achieve salvation. Having tried severe penance, but failing to find an answer through that
means, Siddhartha meditated. After many days of meditation
under the Bodhi Tree (a *pipal* or *ficus religiosa*), he received
the Great Enlightenment and realized the true path to salvation. Buddha preached his first sermon at Sarnath and traveled far and wide with his message, soon developing a large
following of devotees whose numbers swelled enormously
with time. Eventually, Buddhists were divided into two sects,
the *Mahayana* (progressive branch) and the *Hinayana* (orthodox branch).

The main object of Buddhism is to achieve *nirvana,* or
salvation, through the obliteration of pain, which in turn is to
be achieved through the obliteration of desire. Buddha's

teachings are embodied in the Four Noble Truths and the Eightfold Path:

The Four Noble Truths: The world is full of suffering; suffering is caused by desire; renunciation of desire leads to *nirvana*, or salvation; and salvation can be achieved by following the eightfold path.

The Eightfold Path: Right beliefs; right aims; right conduct; right livelihood; right speech; right effort; right thinking; and right meditation.

Buddhism's original appeal lay in the fact that it gave people a way out from under the domination of the Brahmin priests and their abstruse rituals and philosophies. It was a religion with which the common man could free himself and find comfort outside the caste hierarchy. Buddhism had many adherents in India at one time, including some of India's most powerful monarchs who actively propagated it. However, it primarily flourished outside its birthplace as a missionary religion. The appeal of Buddhism has continued through the centuries. Asia's most widespread faith, Buddhism has become very popular today in the West as well, particularly in the United States.

Buddhism was not the only religion to emerge out of the dissatisfaction with Brahminical Hinduism. Vardhamana, known to posterity as Mahavira, a contemporary of Buddha, founded a religion which was also named after him. He was called "*Jina*," which means "*The Conqueror*." Mahavira, like Buddha, was also a prince who left his home and became an ascetic in order to search for the true way to salvation. After thirteen years, having *conquered* his human impulses, he received Enlightenment and spent the rest of his life spreading his message. Mahavira's teachings then came to be called

Jainism. He died by self-starvation, which, according to Jaina doctrine, is the ideal way.

The basic tenets of the Jaina faith are:

1. ***The Universe is composed of animate and inanimate worlds***

2. ***Everything animate (natural) has a soul***

According to Jaina belief, the only way to salvation is through the freeing of the soul. The aim of a person seeking salvation is to release himself from impediments which weigh down his soul. Impediments are caused by wordly attachments. Worldly attachments can only be removed by the observance of right beliefs, right knowledge, and right behaviors. The only right way for an individual is to renounce a world full of ills and decay and to embrace an ascetic and rigorously disciplined life.

An ideal life, according to Jaina tradition, would be that of a monk. In fact, Buddhism and Jainism, through the philosophies of renunciation and withdrawal, created the institution of monasteries in India. Jainism is essentially atheistic and does not seek to proselytize.

The preeminent belief in non-violence in Jainism stems from the tenet that every natural object has a soul. Thus, Jainism believes in complete non-violence towards all living things, no matter how tiny. A common practice among orthodox Jainas is to cover the mouth with a thin piece of gauze so as not to even accidentally inhale any insects. This practice distinctly espresses the fervent Jaina belief in non-violence towards all living things, which dramatically influenced the ancient custom of animal sacrifice in Hinduism. The Hindu belief in *Ahimsa* (non-violence) found the highest status in Jainism (as well as in Buddhism), leading to a decline in the slaughter of animals and thus to vegetarianism, markedly altering the diets of Indians through the centuries.

The monasteries of Buddhists and Jainas were extremely well-funded by their patrons, and became great centers of learning. Both religions have contributed tremendously to the philosophical heritage of India, but this is a subject well beyond the scope of this book. Buddhist and Jaina philosophies, however, remained an oral tradition until the 3rd century B.C. Wealthy Jaina monasteries have also contributed fabulous monuments, some of which are still in existence. Jainism has a large following (particularly in the business communities) in India today. In fact, Gandhi, a Hindu, strictly observed some Jaina tenets. Jainism, like Buddhism, came to have two sects, the *Shwetambara* (the progressive sect) and the *Digambara* (the orthodox sect).

The inaccessibility of the high Brahmanical priesthood led to the birth of yet another religion in the 15th century A.D., when Nanak Deo, the founder of the Sikh faith, rejected pomp and circumstance, striking an important chord among the hardworking artisans and peasants of his land, the Punjab. Nanak embraced people who lived simple lives and who wanted a faith to which they could easily relate without the consequences of caste restrictions. Born a Hindu and brought up by Muslims, Nanak revolted against the orthodoxy of all existing religions and sought to incorporate into one faith the best of all the religions around him. He based his teachings on equality. Being influenced by Bhaktism, Guru ("teacher" as he came to be called) Nanak emphasized personal devotion to one God, and attracted Muslims and Hindus alike.

Guru Nanak did away with burdensome rituals, idol worship, social hierarchy, and the caste structure ruled by Brahmins. *(See Part Two.)* His philosophy became a widely practiced religion, with scriptures and symbols which would distinguish it from other religions. The teachings of Guru Nanak are written in the *Adi Granth*, reverently referred to as the *Granth Sahib*, which was compiled by Guru Arjun Singh in 1604. Nanak's teachings were written in a new script, named *Gurmukhi* after him.

After Nanak there were nine other Sikh Gurus: Guru Angad; Guru Amar Das; Guru Ram Das; Guru Arjun Das (tortured to death by Jehangir); Guru Hargobind; Guru Har Rai; Guru Hari Krishen; Guru Tegh Bahadur (beheaded by Aurangzeb); and his son, Guru Gobind Rai, the tenth and last Guru. Gobind Rai, who lived from 1666-1708, promised to avenge his father's death. Calling himself *Singh,* or "lion," he rallied the Sikhs under the following symbols of unity, all of which begin with the letter *ka* from the Gurmukhi alphabet: *kesh* (long hair); *kanga* (comb); *kirpan* (dagger); *kada* (bracelet); and *kachha* (shorts). The observance of all of the symbols served to unify the Sikhs into a martial community, now named *Khalisa,* or pure. These symbols are observed even today by most Sikhs. Sikhism has adherents all over the world, including the United States of America and Canada.

In addition to the above Indian-born religions, millions of Indians belong to religions such as Islam, Christianity, Judaism, and Zoroastrianism, which have had their origin in other countries.

Islam, one of the major religions of the world, was brought to India from the eleventh century A.D. onwards by the Arabs, Turks, Afghans, and Persians, who came to the country as tradesmen, invaders, and mystics. There are about one hundred million Muslims in India. Like Muslims elsewhere, Indian Muslims belong mainly to two sects, *Shia* and *Sunni*, and observe their holy days in strict accordance with their beliefs. Muslims are a critical ingredient of Indian culture and life, and through the centuries, have contributed profoundly to her history and development. Muslim India has produced some of the world's most beautiful art and architecture as well as outstanding literature. There are mosques and shrines in almost every town in India, and Islamic festivals are observed with aplomb.

India is also home to the *Sufis*, the adherents of a mystical branch of Islam. Sufism, with its mystical and ascetic aspects, appeared in Persia in the tenth century, but arriving in India a couple of centuries later, found a familiar and hospitable climate. It was brought to India by the Sufi *pirs*, or saints. By the thirteenth century these saints had developed a large following, converting people to their faith by persuasion rather then force. All over India today, shrines which command the most passionate gatherings are those of the *pirs*, and their *urs* (special days) are celebrated with tremendous fanfare and enthusiasm. The music at these gatherings is unrivaled in its ability to move the audience and usually takes the form of *qawwalli* (devotional chorus). In Kashmir, the fusion of the Sufi and Bhakti movements produced a new type of Sufism, called the *Rishi* order which included both Muslims and Hindus. Kashmir is thus frequently referred to by the Kashmiris as *"Rishi-var,"* or the valley of the Rishis.

Christianity, another religion which found followers in India, is accorded several possible routes and sources for its arrival. Some trace Christianity in India to 52 when it is said that St. Thomas, apostle of Christ, was brought to India. It is believed that he toured the country, set up churches until he met opposition in the south, and was martyred in Mylapore. His followers are called Syrian Christians. Other groups think it more likely that Christianity came by sea to Kerala on the southwestern coast of India and that there were small groups of Christians there by the year 600. Then, of course, there have also been conversions through the centuries due to the proselytizing efforts of the Christian missionaries who accompanied the Europeans. These missionaries have contributed some of the finest educational institutions in India, which they still maintain.

Judaism was brought to India by early Jewish traders, and there is some evidence which suggests that the first Jews to arrive in India might have come in the first century A.D. However, other evidence points to a later date, the 10th century, when a Jewish community settled in Kerala under the protection of a local chieftain. In any event, Jews have continued since then to make India their home, particularly Jews from the Middle East and Europe. Today, the Jewish community in India is composed of three main groups: the Bene Israel (which is the largest); the Cochini; and the Baghdadi. The Jewish community is very small and is concentrated in Cochin, Bombay, and a few other towns in the south. The Indian Jews observe their rituals very strictly, but as with other religions, local customs have crept into some of their traditions.

The Jews were not alone in being promised protection in India. Zoroastrianism was brought to India between the seventh and the eighth centuries by Persian refugees fleeing Muslim persecution. Zoroastrians are named after their Teacher, Zoroaster or Zarathustra. India has the largest number of

Zoroastrians (called Parsis) in the world although there are still a few in Iran and some in Pakistan. The Parsi community has contributed some of India's most patriotic sons and daughters, politicians, and industrialists. The Parsis have also picked up some new traditions while faithfully preserving their ancient rituals and customs. They are well-known for their philanthropy.

In conclusion, India is mainly Hindu with about eleven percent of her population composed of Muslims. The other religions in India are (in order of numbers) Christians, Sikhs, Buddhists, Jainas, Zoroastrians, Jews, and other faiths.

Although India's constitution is secular (non-religious), all major religious days are accorded equal respect, and the entire nation, regardless of one's religion, observes these days as holidays. Thus, Indians celebrate Hindu festivals such as *Diwali* (at which lamps are lit and sweets are distributed) and *Dassehra* (at which effigies of epic villains are set ablaze). Muslim holy days such as *Id-ul-fitr* (to mark the end of *Ramzan*), *Id-ul-zuha* (to commemorate Ibrahim's sacrifice in accordance with the wishes of God), and *Muharram* (which remembers the martyrdom of Imam Husain) are also observed by the whole nation. In addition, the nation observes *Gurpurab* (Guru Nanak's birthday), Christmas, Good Friday, Mahavira *Jayanti* (birthday of Mahavira), and Buddha *Jayanti* (birthday of Buddha), also called Buddha *Purnima*. Thus, when I am asked which is the major holiday for Indians, I am at a loss to answer the question!

As a Kashmiri Hindu, my most important celebration is *Sivaratri* (the union of Siva and his consort), but the same is not true of all Hindus. Local religious festivals differ from region to region and are too numerous to list here. Among the most interesting ones are the Buddhist festival of the Hemis *Gumpha* (monastery), held in the Himalayan heights at Ladakh, and the *Rath Yatra* (chariot ride) at Puri in Orissa at which devotees pull a gigantic chariot carrying Lord Jagannatha (an event which gave birth to the English word "juggernaut").

In addition to the above religious festivals, days of historic importance are also national holidays. The 26th of January (Republic Day), the 15th of August (Independence Day), and the 2nd of October (Gandhi *Jayanti*) are among the historical days observed throughout the nation. Of the historical celebrations, the Republic Day Parade is probably one of the most spectacular in the world. A ceremonial procession goes down the promenade from the *Rashtrapati Bhavan,* or Presidential Palace, to the India Gate (a monument which honors Indian soldiers killed in World War II). The procession includes armed tanks, marching troops, children and folk dancers, camels, tribal splendor, and farmers dressed in rural costumes. This ends with a fly-past by Indian Air Force planes which leave a trail of orange, green, and white in the sky representing the Indian tricolor flag.

The cultural diversity of India can also be found in its regional holidays which differ from region to region and are based on a variety of themes. Thus, the south has harvest festivals called *Pongal* and *Onam*, and the north has spring festivals called *Lodi* and *Basant*. Some festivals are left over from feudal times, such as *Raksha Bandhan*, when girls tie *rakhis,* or beautiful talismans, on their brothers (or proxy brothers) and ask them to be brave in their endeavors. In return, the brothers promise to take care of their sisters. This dates back to the time when women tied talismans on the men who were going to war. In some parts of India, men tie a *rakhi* on women as well. In a spring festival called *Holi*, people go to friends' houses, hiding colored powder in their hands behind their backs. When the door is opened, the willing hosts allow their faces to be smeared with red, yellow, and green powder, signifying the colors of spring. The colors wash off easily, and everyone settles down to some tea and sweets.

Some Indian festivals celebrate animals, such as the camel, the bullock, and the elephant. These animals have been an important part of the lives of Indians since the Indus Valley Civilization. The Pushkar fair held in Rajasthan is the world's largest camel fair, and camels are bought and sold and exhibited here. At this fair, the most spectacular human dances may also be seen and riveting music heard. Some villages have hair-raising bullock cart races. Elephants have been honored through time in India as wartime help and peacetime beasts of burden and are still used for transportation today. Not surprisingly, therefore, elephant festivals are held with great fanfare in some parts of India. As with religious festivals, very few secular festivals are common to all parts of the country.

Most festivals in India are of religious provenance. However, the most valuable and enduring by-product of India's romance with religion has been the art and architecture which can be found throughout the country. Whether one is talking about temples or mosques, the fine arts or the performing arts, religion has provided the inspiration for India's rich heritage. Secular themes in Indian art developed mainly after the sixteenth century, but the influence of religion is much older and all pervasive in classical Indian art and architecture.

CHAPTER TWELVE

What is the educational system in India ?

Since time immemorial education has been accorded the highest place in the lives of Indians. The earliest educational system is the one we know about from the literature of the ancients. The Dharmashastras, for example, prescribed that the first twenty-five years of a person's life be devoted to education, although this was not universally applied. However, it does show the importance accorded to education. The two epics, the *Ramayana* and the *Mahabharata*, for example, illustrate the integral part that teachers and training played in the lives of the epic protagonists. It is obvious from ancient treatises that young students entered the *gurukul* (boarding school) under the supervision of the *guru* (teacher) where they learned arts and sciences. It seems that they would leave their parents' comfortable homes for the privilege of being under the tutelage of the guru in an *ashram,* or ascetic cottage. In the centuries to follow, after attending the *Gurukul*, those who wanted to pursue further studies would then go to a university. The universities of ancient India, such as Varanasi, Taxila, Ajanta, Ujjain, and Nalanda, attracted scholars from all over the world. Those who gained admission were given free board and lodging. If less academic pursuits were desired, vocational education could be obtained at the guilds, which were the centers of technical knowledge.

The educational institutions for arts and sciences in India were rivaled by few, and thus they attracted scholars from around the world. India was far ahead of the Greeks in every field of mathematics except geometry. Numerals were borrowed by the Arabs from India and later introduced to the world as *Arab* numerals. India is also the birthplace of the zero as well as the decimal system, which was well-established there by the 6th century A.D. Interestingly, algebra was developed independently by both Greece and India. In India algebra was further developed by Aryabhatta (476-550). He was one of the first people in the world to use algebra, and certainly the first to write algebra in verse form! Although the debt to Greece in astronomy was well acknowledged by Indian astronomers, particularly by Aryabhatta and Varahamihira (505-587), their work shows that the Indians were masters in their own right. Brahmagupta (598-665) and Bhaskara (1114-1185) were heads of observatories, and masters of astronomy, astrology, and mathematics.

India was far advanced in comparison to Europe in the medical sciences as well. The earliest compendium of medical knowledge from India is attributed to Charaka, the court physician of Kanishka, in the first century after the birth of Christ. Some of this ancient medical knowledge, such as *Ayurvedic* medicine (from the *Ayur Veda* or medical treatises), has continued to be respected through the millennia and is currently enjoying a rebirth today in the world of alternative and holistic medical sciences. Herbs as a source of medicines, prophylactics, and anesthesia are also mentioned repeatedly in the ancient textbooks. The other great Indian physician of antiquity was Sushruta who lived around the fifth century A.D. He wrote a book on medicine, described anesthesia, used cadavers for research, performed plastic and other surgery, used a large assortment of surgical instruments as well as antiseptics, and practiced hypnotism. Indian surgeons of antiquity are credited with being the first plastic surgeons because they performed reconstructive surgery on the unfortunate recipients of a common form of punishment, i.e., cutting off the tip of the nose. Thus, rhinoplasty, as this surgery is called today, must have been a lucrative practice for an aspiring doctor to consider. It is important to remember that doctors were not regarded as magicians in ancient India because they had formal training in the healing arts, and their knowledge was based on empirical evidence. The people of ancient India also had the benefit of being the owners of the earliest sex manual known to man, the *Kama Sutra,* written by Vatsyayana around the first or second century A.D.

India was well advanced in the metallurgical sciences and the application of iron and steel, evidence of which can be seen in some ancient temples. An iron pillar, which stands untarnished in New Delhi after fifteen centuries, provides solid proof of the advanced level of applied metallurgy in India at that time.

It is quite clear that India pursued learning with great vigor in ancient times. What about today? Unfortunately, the literacy level and education in India suffered a decline with the passage of time and a severe setback under the British period. Traditional forms of education gradually withered away, and nothing was done to replace them. Then Thomas Babington Macaulay, Lord Bentinck's Law Member in 1835, was charged with the task of filling the vast gap between British masters and their Indian subjects. He created a class of Western-educated Indians who were able (and what is more important, willing) to serve the Crown. He succeeded in this task admirably for a while until this class of Indians answered a higher call and joined the freedom movement. The masses, however, continued to be deprived of educational opportunities. (*See Chapter Five.*)

During the British rule, some Indians did try under difficult circumstances to bring back the importance of education which had been such a critical ingredient of Indian culture. For example, Pandit Madan Mohan Malaviya revived the ancient university of Varanasi, naming it the Benares Hindu University. Similarly Sir Syed Ahmed Khan set up the Aligarh Muslim University. Both of these universities provided an alternative to the limited educational opportunities being offered at that time to Indians. Needless to say, these attempts did not even begin to address the problem.

Fortunately, of all the strides made by post-independence India, none is greater than its progress in the field of education. Approximately fifty percent of Indians are literate, and while this does not sound like a very high figure, it is useful to remember that the literacy rate has doubled in the last fifty years since India achieved independence. Even so, much remains to be done, particularly for women.

Today, in most parts of India, public education is free and accessible to children up to the college level. Children go to primary school at about six years of age and graduate from high school at about seventeen. Some small villages do not have schoolhouses, and teachers simply hold their classes under the shade of a tree. In these village schools, classes are postponed in case of inclement weather. Children also have the choice of studying at a private school. Regardless of all the varying conditions under which their schooling takes place, Indian children must pass a qualifying examination before they can enter college. This secondary examination is regulated by the State Board of Education and is uniform for all students under the Board's jurisdiction.

Education is basically in the hands of the state government with the central government playing a coordinating and policy-planning role. The Government of India also regulates universities and colleges in India. There are several private colleges as well. Quite a few of the private colleges are run by Christian missions and other parochial agencies. The degree examinations for all higher educational institutions are standardized statewide. In recognition of the need for training in the fields of modern management and business, several state-of-the-art Institutes of Management have also been established in different parts of India.

In addition to liberal arts institutions there are many vocational (or "polytechnic") schools as well as regional engineering colleges in all the states. The Indian Institute of Technology, patterned after the Massachusetts Institute of Technology, consists of five prestigious engineering schools located in Delhi, Kanpur, Madras, Kharagpur, and Bombay. Similarly, there are regional medical colleges in the states and several Institutes of the Sciences located in the different parts of the country. In fact, India has the third largest number of scientists and engineers in the world, after the United States of America and the former Soviet Union.

It is heartening to see that education has rapidly regained the preeminence it had in the lives of Indians, who are very eager for college and university degrees. In fact, this great desire for an advanced level of education in a poor country creates a situation where there are a large number of educated people who are unemployed or underemployed. By and large, though, India's preoccupation with education has proven to be a great boon, creating the largest educated workforce in the world, a workforce which has a great competitive edge in today's job market. *(See Chapter Thirteen.)*

What is the Indian economy?

In spite of its centuries-old history as a wealthy land, India is described today as a developing, or poor, country. There are several reasons for this. We have already gone through some of India's economic history in Chapter Five. However, while the past has certainly played its part in the economic condition in which India finds herself today, there are some problems and issues affecting the economic status of India which have arisen in the fifty years since she became independent.

At the dawn of her independence, India was faced with the monumental task of pulling out of a colonial past and into the twentieth century. This meant the social, political, and economic reconstruction of India from a subject country into a sovereign nation which would retrieve its historical place among the nations of the world. The social and political aspects have been discussed in other chapters. Here we shall try to take a look at the economy of India.

The leaders of newly-independent India felt that India's economy, after years of exploitation and backwardness under the British, could not be left to chance or private initiative. It was decided that the Government of India had to set the Indian economy on a path which would ensure progress and at the same time benefit the greatest numbers. Hence, a "planned" economy was decided upon, one which would be managed by a series of government-formulated Five-Year Plans.

The "planned" Indian economy, based partly on socialistic ideals, was neither entirely state-controlled nor entirely privately-owned, but a cumbersome "mix" of both types. Thus, the economy was divided into three sectors: the public (the largest sector which includes projects dealing with "critical" areas); the private (a smaller, more consumer-goods-oriented sector); and the joint sector (a collaborative effort between private enterprise and the government). There was a strong underlying bias against any foreign involvement or control in the Indian economy and a strong bias towards self-reliance. This resulted in severe governmental restrictions and control on international trade, particularly on importing goods from other countries.

This controlled or government-managed approach to development did achieve its aim of developing a diversified industrial base in India. Traditional Indian industry, i.e., metal, wood, tanning, dyeing, glass, etc., in existence since antiquity, was now joined by other modern industries such as heavy machinery, electronic equipment, engines, nuclear facilities, pharmaceuticals, and textiles, to mention a few. India's iron and steel industry has existed since the beginning of this century, but it expanded to its present imposing status only after independence. Almost all the computers, cars, and refrigerators in use in the nation are Indian-made, a fact which always surprises visitors. At any rate, India's multi-faceted industrial foundation proved to be invaluable to her economic growth, and placed India among the top industrial nations of the world.

The Five-Year Plans initially put India on a sound economic footing, but they rapidly became outdated and outpaced. The fact was that the government of such a large and impoverished country simply did not have the resources to manage a major portion of the economy. Moreover, the post-independence fear of foreign control and preoccupation with self-reliance became outdated in the face of contemporary global economic realities. As a result, India's share of world trade, as well as her own economy, shrank drastically, almost leading her to economic disaster. Then, in 1991 the government shifted away from its earlier approach of the strict compartmentalization of sectors (discussed earlier in this chapter) and began the liberalization of the economic policies of India.

As a result of these new liberalization policies, the government began to remove restrictions, freeing the economy to incorporate changes critical to bringing it more in line with forthcoming needs of the twenty-first century. Thus, some formerly government-controlled areas are now in private hands, and for the most part licensing restrictions and bureaucratic meshes have been removed from the path of entrepreneurial efforts. Both of these developments have resulted in the mushrooming of private enterprise in India. The restrictions on international trade are also being eliminated, removing the damaging isolation of India from the global economy and restoring some of her forgotten status as a well-known trading nation around the world.

However, India faces another major problem which needs to be addressed. Any discussion of the economy of India, a country which holds a fifth of the world's population, must begin with the acknowledgment of the fact that India's population explosion has serious implications. Approximately one-third the size of United States, India today has a population which is growing at the rate of nineteen million people a year. At this rate, India is fast approaching a population of a billion people. It is a sobering thought and one to be kept in mind when examining India's economy, that at the present rate of growth the next century will see India surpass China as the world's most populous nation.

Naturally, India is engaged in trying to limit the formidable rate of her population growth *within* her democratic framework. There has been some success in popularizing birth control methods throughout the urban and rural areas. This is a much-needed strategy because in an agrarian society with low life-expectancy levels, larger families have always seemed to make more economic sense. Through its various Health and Family Planning programs, the government has tried to change these age-old attitudes in order to stem the tide of growing humanity in India. However, although an impressive slowing down in the birth rate has been achieved, India has not really been able to show any dramatic rates of population decline in terms of numbers. One of the major contributing reasons for this is the fact that the mortality rate in India has declined faster than the declining birth rate.

The fact remains, of course, that the problem of population growth cannot be solved by the government alone. There is hope that education, particularly among women, will hasten the people's own initiative to slow down the birth rate. This hope is based on the experience of Kerala, a state with a literacy rate of over 90 percent among women, which has the lowest birth rate in the country, a rate which is far below the national rate. The daunting fact is that in spite of the doubling of literacy since India's independence, one-half of the population above fifteen years of age and two-thirds of the women over the age of fifteen are still illiterate. It is, therefore, obvious that educating the public in matters of health is not an overnight process and will take time, and this is an enormous problem for the economic outlook for the country.

The health sector in India is under the jurisdiction of the states of the federation, but the national policy planning takes place in the Union Government, which plays a vital role in health programs across the country. National programs have been initiated to combat or eradicate diseases and to create health education schemes such as the family planning programs. The Union Government also plans for sanitation, water supply, and nutrition. Thanks to the aggressive efforts of these programs, life expectancy in India has doubled since 1947. However, as things stand today, in spite of an army of able and qualified doctors, most public health care services in India suffer from a tremendous lack of resources and leave much to be desired. It is important to remember that this results from the fact that most public health care services are free for those who cannot afford private care. Again, overwhelming population pressure creates demands that simply cannot be met. This is a particularly alarming fact to consider in view of the long-term care required for AIDS patients, whose numbers are increasing ominously in India.

The population figures also have had a serious impact on the agricultural sector, which is the largest sector in India's economy. Ironically, even though half of her land was cultivated, India continued to experience severe shortages in food supply in the early decades after independence. In fact, India could not feed her people. These problems with agricultural output were the result of centuries of neglect and abuse of the agricultural sector discussed in Chapter Five. Then, in the late sixties, India modernized her ancient agricultural practices, a change which was termed the "Green Revolution" under which the country was introduced to high-yielding hybrid wheat and rice seeds and new agricultural technology.

This program proved to be a turning point for India's food problem. The agricultural deficit was turned into a surplus; self-sufficiency in foodgrains was attained; and the Indian economy received a much-needed boost.

In spite of innovations such as the Green Revolution, the Indian agricultural system remains largely traditional with the monsoons still playing a critical role in the harvest. Until very recently only the state of Punjab had a history of trying strenuously to develop other forms of irrigation, such as the canal system and tubewells. These efforts made the Punjab the "breadbasket" of India and her richest agricultural state. Other states have now implemented improved schemes for their own agricultural development with very impressive results in all agricultural spheres, particularly in the area of crop yields.

The two main food crops of India are rice and wheat, which form the staple of Indian diets. Both crops are grown for domestic consumption as well as for export. Among the other crops grown in India are sugarcane, millets, pulses, oilseeds, spices, tea, coffee, rubber, and jute (of which India is the world's largest producer). India has the largest livestock population in the world. However, poor stock quality and lack of good feed have resulted in very poor milk yields. Attempts are underway to crossbreed indigenous cattle with high-yielding milch cattle from other parts of the world.

Fortunately, famines now seem to be a thing of the past, but the average daily caloric intake in India is low. Although food production and distribution have made huge jumps since independence and the standard of living has improved, income distribution in India is still not as equitable as it should be. Income disparities are huge between the rich and the poor, and malnutrition is a widespread problem for the simple reason that many millions of Indians live below the poverty line.

Sandwiched between the rich and the poor is the middle class (the world's largest middle class), which is growing all the time, thanks to the freeing up of the Indian economy. Placed at around 250 million strong, roughly the size of the entire population of the United States, the affluent middle class in India makes her the world's fifth-largest economy in terms of purchasing power parity. Nevertheless, the per capita income in India is much lower than that of other countries which have comparable industrial development. It is hoped that the liberalization of the economic policies, which seem to have influenced all sectors of the Indian economy, will eventually lead to an increase in per capita income.

One of the other sectors benefiting from the new policies is banking. India inherited a highly-developed credit system from her ancient past although some modern banking was introduced by the British. Now India enjoys the benefits of a state-of-the-art banking system which enables her to deal with national and international business in a burgeoning economy. Although the largest banks in India have been nationalized, several international banks have also opened up offices in today's India. All banking activity is regulated by the Reserve Bank of India. These developments in the financial sector augur well for India's economic future.

Anxiety about the economic future of India cannot be attributed to any lack of indigenous resources, for India is well-endowed with mineral resources and great reserves of coal, iron ore, manganese ore, bauxite, etc. In fact, India is one of the world's largest iron ore exporters. However, for many years India's balance of payments position was very weak due to her reliance on imported oil and other imports. This reliance still exists although it has been considerably reduced by such factors as repatriated hard currency and increased domestic oil and natural gas production. Since we are talking about currency, this seems a good place to answer another often-asked question: "What is the monetary unit in India?" India's currency is called the rupee which is equal to a hundred paise. At the time of writing, a dollar is worth about thirty rupees.

While talking about resources, one must also mention manpower, a resource in which India is very rich indeed. The population explosion may spread the benefits of economic growth thinly, but the value of manpower as a resource cannot be underestimated. Thus, labor-intensive industries have been suggested as one of the ways to bring about economic change in India. In addition to her labor force, India also has the largest technical workforce as well as the largest number of college graduates in the world. As a result, India is fast advancing in the electronics and communications business. Many Indian engineers working abroad are returning to India to set up software and hardware companies, helping India to become well prepared to meet the challenges of the twenty-first century.

The Indian Government's efforts to change the economy has affected energy, another of its "critical" sectors (i.e., one which was earlier kept out of private hands). India's main sources of energy are thermal and hydroelectric power, most of which have been developed since 1947. India also derives energy from nuclear plants and has large sources of natural gas, which have only now begun to be tapped. Kerosene, natural cooking gas, and electric power are the most commonly-used domestic energy sources in the urban areas. In spite of these developments, cow dung and firewood, which are the traditional forms of fuel for rural domestic consumption, continue to be used by most Indians because they are the least expensive. Cow dung is also used now to produce bio-gas or methane for fuel. In a land where the sun is plentiful and a dominant factor, attempts are also being made to harness solar energy, but this industry is still in an embryonic stage.

As things stand today, the energy output in India can hardly keep pace with rapidly-growing demand, and the need for improvement in this area cannot be overstated. There are frequent breakdowns and shortages due to various reasons such as overload, equipment defects, and so on. Projects to increase India's energy output are now being undertaken by foreign private concerns in collaboration with private and governmental Indian companies. In due course these should give Indians a dependable and continuous source of energy.

International collaboration in all areas of economic activity has multiplied as India in the nineties opens up rapidly to international investments. The fact that English is the *lingua franca* in India has been a tremendous asset in helping her presence in international business. The international business community also seems to be comfortable with the fact that India is a democracy which operates under a Western judicial system and on the principle of the rule of law. This element of familiarity and predictability in India's system seems to appeal to international, particularly Western, nations.

In addition to the English language, the British have, however inadvertently, left behind some other assets which have aided India in today's world. One such asset is the rail-

way system. Almost all of the 40,000 miles of railway originated under the British *Raj*, and this mileage makes the Indian railway system the fourth largest in the world, after the
U.S.A., the former U.S.S.R., and Canada. After independence
India made major investments in modernizing, maintaining,
and improving this valuable legacy although here again the
population pressure bears down heavily on the efficacy of the
railway system.

Another inheritance from the British period in India was
the Indian Civil Service, a huge, anachronistic bureaucratic
machinery, which had served the *Raj* well when the well-
being of the common man was not a top priority. *(See Part
Two.)* After independence, this bureaucracy, renamed the Indian Administrative Service, was given the mandate to serve
the people and to provide continuity and stability for the ongoing implementation of government policies, regardless of
the political complexion of the government. However, the new
service took some time to shake off the complicated and slow
procedures of its colonial past, and for decades it could not
adapt quickly enough to the new economic realities in India.
Fortunately, with the freeing up of the economy in the
nineties, this bureaucratic stranglehold on the economy has
finally been removed. The Indian Administrative Service now
aids India's new economic impetus, playing a vital role in the
formulation and implementation of appropriate policies to
rectify India's economic problems. Its non-partisan and permanent nature, coupled with its new attitude towards the
economy, make it an invaluable resource.

In conclusion, India may be classified as a developing,
Third World, or poor country, but she is in fact a curious mix
of poverty on the one hand and a wealth of resources not usu-

ally found in poor countries on the other. As described above, this wealth is found in a well-developed industrial base, a well-developed infrastructure, many natural resources, the largest pool of highly-qualified English-speaking technical men and women in the world, a Western legal system which operates on the principle of the rule of law, and finally in a trained career civil service which is permanent and non-partisan. With these strengths in place, it seems that the business climate in India is once again, after centuries, conducive to profitable enterprise, a development which holds tremendous hope for her economic future.

Part Two

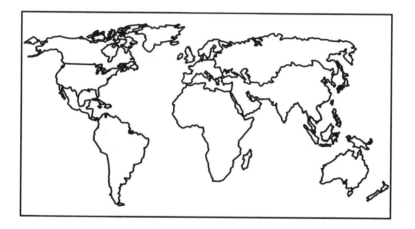

How about some historical dates?

The following is a chronology from ancient times to the present, a continuum based on interesting and important dates related to the history of India. Periods from prehistoric and early historic times are approximations as it is impossible to give exact dates for these.

Chronology:

–400,000 –200,000	The earliest signs of human life in the subcontinent of India
–6000	Agriculture in India
–5000	Agricultural settlements in Egypt and Sumer
–4000	Wheel and plough in Mesopotamia
–4000–3000	Some settlements in northern India
–3500–3000	The development of wedge-shaped cuneiform, earliest known writing, in Mesopotamia
–2950	Growth of civilization in Indus Valley
–2500	Indus Valley Civilization, also known as Harappan Culture; trade between Harappans and Mesopotamia
–1600	Arrival of Aryan tribes, also called Indo-Europeans, in the north of India

This arrival is part of a dispersal of the Aryan tribes from their homeland, which archaeologists have still not determined in 1997; south Russia and Central Asia are widely regarded as probable homelands. The Aryans receive their name from their language, not their race. They carry their language with them, and this is one way that the world has come to know of their migration. Thus, treaties and other records from this period (or earlier) in Mesopotamia reveal names of deities such as Surya, Indra, Maruta, and in Anatolia (today's Turkey), names such as Indra and Varuna. These names are identical to their Sanskrit counterparts in India where they are popular names to this day!

−1500 End of the Indus Valley Civilization and establishment of the Aryans in northern India

−1500–1000 Vedic Aryans in India

The Aryans are now called Vedic by historians because this is the period when they begin the composition of the Vedas, the most ancient texts of Hinduism. The Rg Veda is the earliest Veda, and the caste system is first mentioned here. The Vedic gods are similar to the nature gods of heaven, water, air, and earth found in Europe. Vedism eventually absorbs indigenous beliefs prevalent in the Indian subcontinent, and this entire body of beliefs becomes Hinduism.

\> Silk in China

The silk-moth is believed to have come from east India, but it owes its fame to the ingenuity of the Chinese who discover the potential of the cocoon as a textile source.

−1000 Introduction of rice cultivation from the east to central and western India

−1000–500 Spread of Aryans to the eastern heartland of India; the development of the Ganges civilization in the Gangetic plains

>	Completion of the Vedas

> Varanasi, one of the oldest living cities in the world, in existence as a seat of learning, industry and wealth; one of the seven cities held sacred by Hindus

The university at Varanasi is revived in 1916 as Benares Hindu University by Pandit Madan Mohan Malaviya, a scholar and leader. (My husband and my father both studied at the modern Engineering Colleges there.) The city of Varanasi has been a center of Hindu scholarship since time immemorial.

-900–800 Writing of *Iliad* and *Odyssey* by Greek poet Homer

> Existence of Indraprastha, mythological ancestor city of Delhi

The word Delhi (Dilli) *also means "heartland," and literature and phrases develop through the centuries around the word* Dilli, *a fact which denotes its status at the center stage of Indian politics under many dynasties.*

-800 Use of iron in India, probably earlier

-700–600 Kharoshti and Brahmi, two scripts in use in India

Brahmi becomes the mother of all Indian scripts except Urdu. Brahmi and Kharoshti are traced to Aramaic, a Semitic script which may have reached India through traders.

-600–460 Period of Mahavira Jina, founder of Jainism

> Period of Prince Siddhartha, founder of Buddhism, known to the world as Gautama, the *Buddha* (the Enlightened One), *Sakya Muni (*Ascetic of the Sakya clan)

>	Ujjain in central India as center of government, commerce and colleges, continues for a millennium
−510	First Roman Republic and the beginnings of the Roman Empire, which will last for almost a millennium
−500−400	Nalanda in Bihar, a university as we know it, i.e., lecture rooms, dormitories, and international scholars
−500	Achaemenid Persian conquest of parts of the northern Indian Frontier
−494	Rise of the first major north Indian kingdom of Magadha, which includes parts of what is now Bihar
>	Ajatashatru's murder of his father Bimbisara, first wealthy and powerful king of Magadha, and patron, devotee and contemporary of Buddha
−493	Ajatshatru, King of Magadha, whose successors will be overthrown by Nandas
−460	Birth in Greece of physician Hippocrates, father of Western medicine

Hippocrates is famous for healing, and his oath of medical ethics followed even today. The ancient Greeks and Indians influence each other in the field of medicine, and other areas as well.

−400−300	Taxila, a prosperous town in northwest India, known among Greeks and others for its colleges
>	Panini's analysis of the Sanskrit language and writing of the *Ashtadhyayi*, a definitive work on the science of grammar

> Silver coins in use in India

–327–325 Invasion of the Punjab by Alexander the Great, who turns back after mutiny

–321 Overthrow of Nandas by Chandragupta Maurya; his reconquering of Macedonian territories in India and founding of the Mauryan dynasty, and the first Indian empire

Most of Chandragupta's political success is credited to Chanakya, his chief minister, also called Kautilya or Vishnugupta. Chanakya compiles the Arthashastra, *which is a guide to a well-run government. It also gives us a detailed insight into contemporary Maurya political and economic conditions, foreshadowing the realism of Machiavelli's* Prince, *which comes many centuries later.*

> Spread of Aryan culture to the south of India during the Mauryan period

Sage Agastya, a legendary figure, is credited with carrying Aryan culture to the south, the exact period is uncertain, but traditionally his journey south is said to have taken place prior to the Maurya rule.

> First detailed description of India written for the Greeks by Megesthenes, Greek Ambassador to Chandragupta Maurya; earlier notes on the subject made by Alexander's entourage

–274–232 Asoka the Great, famous for his conversion to Buddhism and his humanitarian reign

–200–400 A.D. Period of Patanjali, philosopher, the father of the Yoga school of Indian Philosophy, grammarian

Patanjali is the author of Yoga Sutra (*compilation of Yogic thought) and* Mahabhashya, *a grammar as well as a com-*

mentary on his times. The exact period is uncertain and his work may have had other contributors.

–190–130	Indo-Greek kings in northwest India
–184	Beginning of the Shunga dynasty, after the Mauryans
–120	Rise of Satyavahanas in the south; first Deccan empire

The Satyavahana hold over the Deccan lasts until the 3rd century, after which their rule declines under pressure from the Shakas (Scythians rulers in the west).

–100	Replacement of Indo-Greeks in north India by Shakas
>	Great *Stupa* (holy place for Buddhists) in Sanchi
>	Rise of Kalinga Kingdom (today's Orissa) under Kharavela; Kalinga's recovery (from defeat at the hands of Ashoka) after Maurya decline
>	Discovery of sea winds from Persian Gulf to western coast of India by Greek sailor which will prove invaluable to traders in the centuries to come
–72	End of the Shungas
–25–21	Trade missions from India received by Emperor Augustus of Rome

India is a vital post on the East-West trade route.

43	Roman conquest of Britain
52	Legendary arrival of St. Thomas in India

60–248   Rule of Kushan dynasty over north India

During this period, the beautiful Indo-Greek Gandhara (from Qandhar in Afghanistan) School of Sculpture, started earlier, flourishes, featuring Buddhist figures created in the Greco-Roman style.

78   Beginning of Shaka calender; in use along with Gregorian calender in India today

78–144   Kanishka, king of the Kushan dynasty

Kanishka organizes the fourth Great Buddhist Council in Kashmir where Buddhists divide into the Mahayana (or Greater Vehicle, or progressive) and the Hinayana (or Lesser Vehicle, or orthodox) sects. Kanishka's court is famous for its artists and intellectuals. Among these luminaries is Charaka, the court physician, author of the oldest medical textbook in India, and Ashwaghosha, the first playwright on record in India. Chinese Buddhist visitors also travel to Kanishka's court and write prolific reports expressing admiration for the prosperity of Kanishka's reign. The tradition of foreigners writing admiring travelogues of India continues.

100–300   Decline of India's trade with Rome; development of ports in Southeast India for trade to Southeast Asia and China

100   Arrival of Chinese ships on the east coast of India

>   First Buddhist missionaries from India arrive in China

150   Period of King Rudradaman of the Shaka dynasty in western India

200–300   Decline of Satyavahanas after conflict with Shakas

>   The kingdoms of Cholas, Pandyas, and Cheras in the

southern-most part of India flourish, having been in existence at least since Ashoka's time

300–400 The rise of *Bhaktism*, or devotional Hinduism emphasizing a personal relationship between man and deity, which continues to evolve and grow in popularity until the sixteenth century, deeply influencing Hinduism; spread of Hinduism to Vietnam, Indonesia, and other parts of Southeast Asia

> Buddhism officially accepted in China

> Ascendancy of Pallavas in Tamil Nadu

300–500 Gupta Golden, or Classical, Age of India

476–550 Aryabhatta, astronomer, mathematician, and writer

Aryabhatta calculates pi to 3.1416 and the solar year to 365.3586, declares the earth a sphere which rotates on its axis, explains that eclipses are caused by the earth's shadow, and calculates the powers of roots and numbers. He also adapts the Babylonian zodiac and proposes a theory of gravity.

480–500 Overthrow of Guptas by the Huns; Hun control over northwestern India

500 Creation of the *Panchatantra*, folk tales of practical advice popular in India even today, remarkably similar to Aesop's fables

> Continuing creation of Ajanta frescoes, started during Gupta and Vakataka reigns

500–900 Major kingdoms of south India embattled with each other

*The Chalukyas (in the western and central Deccan) take over from the Vakatakas, who took over from the Satyavahanas. The Pandyas of Madurai (whose wealth is a subject for comment by Megesthenes and **fifteen centuries** later by Marco Polo) and the Pallavas are the other two kingdoms engaged in the struggle for dominance in the south. By the end of the ninth century, the Cholas take over from the Pallavas. These kingdoms are also patrons of art and literature and contribute several unsurpassed temples to the heritage of India. The imposing rock and shore temples at Mahabalipuram are built by Pallava kings Narsimha Varman I and II in the seventh century. Art and architecture flourish in India under both the Pallavas and the Cholas, and the impact of both is felt in Southeast Asia where it can still be seen in the magnificent ruins of legendary temples.*

505–587 Varahamihira, astronomer and astrologer

Varahamihira's Panchasiddhantika, *or a* Manual on the Five Schools of Astronomy, *indicates Indian knowledge of Greek astronomy.*

542 Death of Mihirgula the Hun in Kashmir

543–757 First line of Chalukyas (of Badami)

550 Buddhism introduced to Korea and Japan

570–651 Bhartihari, philosopher, poet, and grammarian

600–700 First Christian communities in India

600–1000 Spread of Bhakti, a devotional cult, to the north by Nayanars and Alvars (reforming Hindu poets from the South)

The Bhakti Movement seeks to bring god closer by personification and emphasizes devotion to the personified deity rather than an abstract concept. This simple faith becomes popular, and many Hindus return to the fold from Buddhism and Jainism.

606   Sri Harsha Vardhana of the Pushyabhuti dynasty, ruler of a vast empire with its capital at Kannauj, philanthropist, playwright

Harsha is regarded as a just and intellectual king who travels through his kingdom, attending to his subjects and giving donations. His courtier Banabhatta writes the literary masterpiece Kadambari, *as well as a history of Harsha's reign.*

610–642   Defeat of Harsha by Pulakesin II of the Chalukyas; friendly relations between Pulakeshin and Persia

622   Beginning of the Islamic Calendar with the *Hejira*, or the flight of Prophet Mohammed, from his birthplace Mecca to the city of Medina

Mecca and Medina are the two holiest cities for Muslims

625   Systematization of astronomy by Brahmagupta, the Indian mathematician and astronomer at Ujjain

629   Arrival in India of Huen Tsang, the Chinese Buddhist traveler

Huen Tsang studies at the University in Nalanda in Bihar. A nobleman and scholar, Huen Tsang lives at Harsha's court for many years and leaves a detailed account of daily life and the workings of the empire. He describes high intellectual standards and general well-being among the people although petty crime seems to be fairly prevalent.

For those interested in trivia, Huen Tsang mentions the regular use of toothbrushes, probably made from neem *trees, among Indians. The* neem *tree, or* margosa, *is a potent source of medicines and is used all over the world for dental creams today. Even now most Indians brush their teeth with a soft twig from a* neem *tree. One end is chewed into a mop-*

like brush, creating a toothbrush-and-toothpaste-in-one. In the twentieth century Lala Lajpat Rai, a leader of the national movement, refers to these centuries-old standards of personal hygiene when exhorting Indians to consider themselves superior to their British rulers, whom, he says, have only just made the bath a daily ritual!

641	Islam in Persia, leading to the persecution of Zoroastrians and their migration to India
650	Hindu Empire in Sumatra
659	Chinese protectorate in Kashmir and Afghanistan
674	Arrival of Arabs in the Sindh area in the northwest of India
700	Rock cave temples at Ellora, western India, started under the Guptas, continue to be built under other rulers
700–800	Settling of Zoroastrians in central India where they are called *Parsis* because they come from Persia and their language is *Farsi* or Persian

Chess is attributed to this period although its origin was probably earlier when the Persians first came into contact with India. The Persian word for chess is Shatranj, which comes from the Sanskrit word Chaturang, or four angles or divisions.

700–800	Lalitaditya, of the Karkota dynasty, King of Kashmir

Defeating the Arabs in the Sindh, and conquering territories upto Kannauj, Lalitaditya creates a great empire. After his death, however, Kashmir shrinks approximately to the size of the Kashmir Valley. Lalitaditya is considered an outstanding monarch.

> Rise of the Rashtrakutas in the Deccan, the Gurjara Pratiharas in the north and northwest

700–1100 Rule in the east (today's Bengal) by Palas

The rise of Tantricism, a cult with secret rituals and esoteric practices, is associated with the Buddhist Pala period although the cult has existed since the Gupta times. Tantricism influences both Hinduism and Buddhism and probably has roots in the beliefs surrounding deities found at the Indus Valley Civilization, i.e., the male god and the mother goddess.

724 Establishment of Arab authority in the Sindh

725 Bede's introduction of the Christian calendar

757–975 Rule in western and central Deccan by Rashtrakutas

788–840 Reform movement in Hinduism by Shankaracharya, Brahmin philosopher

Traveling all over the country, Shankaracharya seeks to clear up some of the confusions and rituals Hinduism has collected in its long history, proposing knowledge as the only way to salvation. He propounds the Advaita, *or* Monistic, *philosophy and becomes the leading exponent of the* Vedanta *(literally, end of the Vedas) school of philosophy.*

800–900 Vasugupta, teacher and founder of Kashmir School of Saivism

Saivism is the system of beliefs and philosophy followed by the devotees of Siva, one of the gods of the Hindu trinity of Brahma, Vishnu, and Siva.

> Utpala, teacher and exponent of Kashmir Saivism

> Ascendancy of the Cholas in the south

900–1000 Sufism in Persia, which will spread to India from the 11th to the 13th centuries through its *pirs*, or saints

> Chera king welcomes Jew named Joseph Rabban, who establishes Jewish community in Kerala

Some believe the Jews landed on Indian shores much earlier. Trading communities from several religious backgrounds thrive peaceably together on the coastline of India.

939–1020 Firdausi, Persian poet of Ghazni's court

955 Spread of Chola Kingdom after ousting of Pallavas and Pandyas

The Cholas also conquer south India, Ceylon, the Laccadives and the Maldives, and defeat the Southeastern Empire of Sri Vijay. The Cholas exist as a power from the first century and consolidate from the 9th to the 13th centuries with their capital at Tanjore. By the 10th Century, the Cholas are a prosperous kingdom enjoying lucrative trade by sea with the east, including China. They have an impressive navy.

The Cholas fight the second Chalukyas who displace the Rashtrakutas in the tenth century. This leads in the twelfth century to smaller kingdoms in the south, the main ones being the Yadavas (of today's Aurangabad), the Kakatiyas (of today's Andhra) and the Hoysalas (of today's Mysore). Later these kingdoms as well as the Pandyas attack the Cholas. By the end of the 12th Century Chola power is on the decline.

The Pandyas, who have existed in varying strengths since the 4th century B.C., displace the Cholas and rule Tamil Nad from the 13th until the 15th century.

The Chola period sets the standard for the Classical Age in Tamil culture. Chola art in metal, particularly the unmatched bronzes of this period, including the classic Nataraja, are extremely famous and coveted to this day.

975–1189	Rule of second line of Chalukyas (of Kalyani) over Deccan
1000–1030	A number of raids into India conducted by Mahmud of Ghazni, also called Ghazni

Ghazni overruns Kannauj; raids Mathura (a sacred city for Hindus located near Delhi) and Somnath (reputedly the richest Hindu temple at Kathiawar in Gujarat). The regularity with which Ghazni plunders fabled sacred sites is to leave bitter memories among Hindus, Jains, and Buddhists.

1000–1100	*Vetala Panchavimchatika*, stories written about *vetala*, or vampires

My mother used to read me stories about King Vikramaditya and a Vetala, which were serialized in a children's Hindi magazine, many moons ago.

>	Abhinavagupta, philosopher and leading exponent of Kashmir Saivism
1002	Construction of Khajuraho temple complex in Madhya Pradesh in progress

The Khajuraho temples, of which only twenty survive, are famous for their beautiful and erotic sculptures.

1017–1137	Vaishnava philosopher Ramanuja's popularization of the concept of the *love* between a devotee and the deity as a means to salvation, differing from Shankaracharya's belief that *knowledge* alone is the way to salvation

Vaishnavism is the system of beliefs and philosophy followed by devotees of Vishnu of the Hindu trinity of Brahma, Vishnu and Siva.

1030	Alberuni, Arab scholar, in India

1050	Earliest references to Delhi
1070	Expulsion of Cholas by Ceylon
1077	Chola emissaries in China
1100	First universities founded in Europe in Italy and France
>	Jayadeva's *Gitagovinda*, a classical poem of love, dedicated to Lord Krishna
1110	Rise of Hoysala power in Mysore, or *Dorasamudra*, covering central and southern Deccan

The Hoysala dynasty is founded by Vishnuvardana. The Halebid-Belur temples in Mysore are the Hoysalas' major contribution to the heritage of India. The Hoysalas will be replaced by the Vijayanagar kingdom in the fourteenth century.

1110–1200	Decline of Chola power
>	Arrival of Persian words in India with the Turkish invaders; beginnings of Urdu; Hindi already existing as the chief vernacular
>	Probable period of Kalhana's *Rajtarangini*, a classical history of Kashmir
1112	Rise of Anantavarman of the Gajapatis of Orissa who last until the fourteenth century

Anantavarman is said to have built the temple of Jagannath at Puri, around which many legends will evolve. Later Feroz Tughlaq will claim to have destroyed this architectural landmark, which still survives as a prominent place of pilgrimage and tourism.

1150	Hindu Temple of Angkor Vat in Cambodia
1187	Punjab conquered by Mahmud of Ghor, also called Ghori
1192	Prithviraj Chauhan, romantic hero and King of Delhi, defeated and killed by Ghori

I read this story as a young girl, and it has stayed with me. Prithviraj was a dashing prince with whom the princess of Kannauj was in love, but her father, Jaichand, disapproved of him. When her father conducts a swayamvara *(see Index), he shows his contempt of Prithviraj by making an effigy of him as a doorman. However, the princess places the wedding garland around the neck of the effigy, signifying her acceptance of him as her husband. Prithviraj is waiting close by on his steed; he dashes forth; and the lovers escape and get married although history shows that they do not quite live happily ever after.*

1193	Indigo exported to Europe from India
1194	Ghori takes Benares
1199	Ghori takes Kannauj
1200–1300	*Farsi*, or Persian, the court language at the Delhi Sultanate
1200–1400	Rule over Tamil Nad by the Pandyas
1203	Establishment of a kingdom by Ghori in north India at about the same time that Genghis Khan is declared chief prince of the Mongols
1206	Failure of Ghori's plans for consolidation of his kingdom at his death

Ghori's general Qutbuddin Aibak fulfills his dream of establishing a Muslim stronghold over northern India.

> Declaration of the Sultanate of Delhi which lasts from the 13th Century to the 16th Century.

Qutbuddin dies in a polo accident in 1210. The next year his son-in-law Iltutmish succeeds him and makes Delhi the capital.

1215   Magna Carta signed by King John of England, which begins the subordination of the English monarch to the laws of England

1229   Iltutmish's conquest of Bengal

1236   Sultanate most powerful force in northern India

1236–1239   Reign of Razia Sultana, daughter of Iltutmish, the only Muslim sultana, or queen, in Delhi; rule lasts until Razia is murdered

1239–1264   Reign of Narsimha I of Orissa

Narsimha is credited with building the world famous Sun Temple at Konarak in Orissa. Konarak is also famous for its erotic sculptures.

1266–87   Reign of Ghiyasuddin Balban, originally from a Turkish slave family, as the Sultan of Delhi

1271   Journey to China of great Venetian traveler Marco Polo

1288–93   Brief visits by Marco Polo to the coast of India about which he leaves valuable travelogues

Marco Polo and later 15th century travelers take fabulous

stories about the wealth of India back to the West, creating curiosity and greed. Nicolo Conti visits Tungabhadra-Vijayanagar Aqueduct in 1420 and comments on the fact that there are cities all along the Ganges river.

1290 Murder of Kaikobad, Sultan of Delhi; succession of Jalaluddin Khalji

1290–1320 Khalji empire

Jalaluddin Khalji is murdered and replaced by his nephew Allauddin Khalji.

Sultan Allauddin Khalji turns his attentions to the wealthy south in order to find finances for his ambitions. Allauddin defeats the rulers of most of Gujarat, Rajasthan, Andhra, and Tamil Nad, and with the help of his lieutenant Malik Kafur carries legendary riches back to his capital. He is a capable administrator. The south continues to be embattled, with kingdoms rising and falling.

1316 Mubarak, last of Khalji rulers, succeeds Allaudin

He is succeeded by Qutbuddin Mubarak Shah whose murder leads to his succession by Khusro Khan.

1320 Takeover of the Sultanate by the Tughlaqs under Ghiyasuddin Tughlaq

1325 Succession of Muhammed ibn Tughlaq to the Sultanate

> Death of Amir Khusrao Dihlavi, the Indian-born poet, at the age of 72

Khusrao, a student of the Sufi Nizammuddin Aulia, is eminent in the entire world of Persian literature. His mother is Indian, and his father is Turkish. Khusrao, a poet laureate to several monarchs, is the first to write Persian literature in Hindi. He is also the author of some of the earliest Hindi texts. A pioneer of north Indian classical music, he is given the credit for the invention of the sitar *as well as the* tabla.

1325–51

Expansion of the Tughlaq Sultanate to its greatest size under Muhammed ibn Tughlaq

Muhammed ibn Tughlaq tries to establish a second capital at Devagiri (near Aurangabad in the south) now called Daulatabad, all the better to rule his northern and southern territories. This move is a failure, and there is much misery among the dislocated northern populace. The southern rulers throw Muhammed's forces out, and the north is up-in-arms, this is the beginning of his decline.

During Muhammed ibn Tughlaq's reign, Ibn Battutah (1304–1368), the veteran traveler from Tangier, Africa, arrives in Delhi in 1333; he is honored and appointed to a high post for his scholarly talents. He writes an Arabic commentary on his times, an invaluable and objective account of the period.

1338

Declaration of independence from the Delhi Sultanate by Bengal which lasts until its conquest by Akbar in 1576

Other provinces also revolt successfully against Delhi. This fragmentation of the Sultanate into smaller units will make their accession by the Mughals easier.

1345

Establishment by Shamasuddin of the Ilyas Shahi dynasty, which rules Bengal for a century

1346

Founding of the Vijayanagar kingdom over the old Hoysala kingdom

1347

Declaration by Bahman Shah, one of the Deccan Muslim rulers, that he is a Sultan in his own right and independent of Delhi

Bahman Shah establishes the Bahmani Dynasty, which lasts

for two centuries and spends most of its time trying to establish control over the Deccan. However, there is disaffection among the officers of the Bahmani Kingdom, and as a result of this the Vijayanagar Kingdom becomes stronger, particularly under its famous king Krishna Deva Raya, who defeats the Bahmani forces.

1351–88   Reign of Feroz Shah Tughlaq, successor to the Sultanate at Delhi

The Sultanate steadily declines, disintegrates, and falls into complete confusion after Feroz's death. The weak Sultanate is fair game for the next invader.

1368   Ascending of Timur the Lame to the throne of Samarkand in Uzbekistan

1374   Establishment of Vijayanagara Empire which lasts for almost two centuries

1391–94   Rajput princes up-in-arms against Delhi which is in chaos

Rajputana, approximately today's Rajasthan, is the home of the brave Rajput warrior clans and their princes. Rajputana will eventually come under the Mughals and then the Marathas.

1398   Conquest of Delhi by Timur, which reduces the Delhi Sultanate to a fraction of its former size

Timur does not stay to consolidate.

1411–42   Declaration of independence from Delhi by Ahmed Shah in Gujarat

1414–50   Rule of the Sayyids at the Delhi Sultanate after the death of the last Tughlaq

1420–70

The long and eulogized rule of King Zainulabidin, or "Budshah," of Kashmir

Art, architecture, and learning flourish in the valley under Budshah's tolerant and enlightened eye.

1440–1518

Advocacy of moderate spiritualism and asceticism by Kabir Das, member of the Bhakti movement and pioneer of Hindu-Muslim unity

The fourteenth, fifteenth, and sixteenth centuries witness the ascendancy of the Bhakti, or devotee, cult, embodying a personal relationship between deity and devotee. This movement has existed for centuries and has earlier been popularized by the songs of the Tamil saints who were known as the Nayanars and the Alvars. Among the other teachers of this movement are Chaitanya of Bengal (1486–1533), Lalla Ded of Kashmir (14th century), Mirabai of Rajasthan (1503–73), and Sur Das the blind poet (sixteenth century).

Like the Bhakti movement, Sufism places the greatest emphasis on a personal relationship with the Creator, and the two movements influence each other. Among the philosophies of this interaction is that of Kabir Das. Kabir's poems aim at harmony, oneness with God, and Hindu-Muslim unity. He is revered by both religions in his lifetime, and both claim him for their own.

1443

Abdul Razzak, ambassador at the Bahmani Court

Razzak is from Samarkand, the formal capital of Timur. Razzak writes that India is unrivaled among nations.

1451–1526

Restoration of the Delhi Sultanate (except for the kingdom of Rana Sanga of Mewar) to its prior size and glory by the Afghan Dynasty of the Lodis

The Rajputs are a thorn in the side of the Sultanate until the Mughal Emperor Akbar's time when alliances are formed with the Rajputs in the second half of the sixteenth century. Mewar continues to offer resistance to the Mughals.

1469–1538	Guru Nanak Deo, leader and founder of the Sikh religion, disciple of Kabir Das
1492–1504	Voyages of Christopher Columbus to the Americas
1497	Rounding of the Cape of Good Hope by Vasco da Gama, which leads to his discovery of the sea route to India
1498	Arrival of Vasco da Gama in Calicut on the Malabar Coast

Da Gama is warmly welcomed by the Zamorin, or ruler, but the Zamorin is not impressed enough to sign a treaty with him. Calicut (called Kozhikode today) is the birthplace of calico and has had a sophisticated trading community, which includes vast numbers of Arab traders, for centuries. The Portuguese arrival appears to make no significant impact on the minds of Indians at the time.

(This is the same time as Columbus' third voyage to America when he discovers the river Orinoco in Venezuela.).

1500	Arrival of Pedro Alvarez Cabral in Calicut with many ships; subsequent purchase of a warehouse for the Portuguese
1502	Return of Vasco da Gama as a general; his punishment of Indians who murdered the Portuguese who had been left behind in Calicut; establishment of the Portuguese as a force to be reckoned with in the area

Da Gama returns to India with an armed fleet, negotiates with the Zamorin's enemies in Cannanore and Cochin, and indulges in acts of cruelty against the local population of Calicut, particularly the Muslims. By 1503 the Portuguese are a presence in Calicut although they do not establish a stronghold. Goa later becomes the Portuguese center in India.

The Portuguese marry locally to increase their Catholic allies. They also bring potatoes, tomatoes, cashew nuts, green chilies of particular varieties, pineapples, and tobacco, among other items, to India. The Indians are also re-introduced to the fine art of wine-making, and Indian princes prize the horses that the Portuguese import for them.

> Conclusion by Amerigo Vespucci that South America is not India

1509–30   Krishna Deva Raya, famed King of Vijayanagar

Adroit in politics, warfare, and trade, Krishna Deva Raya is a writer, builder, and patron. We have considerable information about his reign from the traveling Portuguese missionary, Domingoes Paes. Raya is friendly with the Portuguese who supply him with much-needed horses for his campaigns.

1510   Dom Affonso d' Albuquerque, founder of eastern Portuguese empire, who seizes Goa from Bijapur and establishes Portugal stronghold there

The cathedral built by Albuquerque in 1511 survives and is still in use.

1525   Invasion of Punjab by Babur who becomes Mughal Emperor

After the first Battle of Panipat in 1526, Babur conquers Delhi and founds the Mughal dynasty in Delhi. The Battle of Panipat is the first step on the road to the fabulous Mughal Empire which lasts until 1761, except for a five-year rule by Sher Shah Suri in 1541. By 1529 Babur's reign extends all over northern India.

1530   Death of Babur; succession of Babur's son Humayun

1532–1623   Tulsi Das, Hindu poet and author of the *Ramcharitmanas*, popular first Hindi version of the epic *Ramayana*

Tulsi Das is influenced by the Bhakti movement.

1542	Reign of Afghan Sher Shah Suri as Sultan of Delhi

> Arrival of St. Francis Xavier (canonized 1602) in Goa

The "Apostle of the Indies" is the first Jesuit missionary in India. Jesuits establish religious and educational institutions in India which carry St. Xavier's name to this day.

1555   Recapture of Punjab, Delhi, and Agra by Humayun

1556   Succession of Humayun's son Akbar (1542–1605)

Akbar's contemporaries are Shakespeare, Elizabeth I, John Calvin, and Galileo Galilei.

After the second Battle of Panipat in 1556, Akbar firmly establishes the Mughal empire. His conquests make a long list, and at his death his reign extends from Kabul in the northwest to the Bengal in the east and from Kashmir in the north to the Deccan in the south.

Akbar makes Farsi the only official court language.

1560   Catholic Luso-Indians (Indian-Portuguese) in Goa under the Spanish Inquisition

1564   Defeat of the Vijayanagar Empire by the alliance formed by the sultans of Bijapur, Golconda, Ahmednagar, Bidar, and Berar (formerly states of the old Bahmani kingdom)

By the end of the seventeenth century these states, except the growing Maratha territories, come under the Mughal Empire.

1570–1620   Firishta, one of the greatest chroniclers of the history of India, particularly that of the Deccan

1573	Meeting of Akbar with a Portuguese delegation to his court
1574	Golden Temple of the Sikhs being built at Amritsar
1579–1586	Yusuf Shah Chak, king of Kashmir, romantic figure in Kashmiri literature

Yusuf and Habba Khatoon are legendary lovers in Kashmir. Habba Khatoon's poems form the heart of many Kashmiri songs.

1580	Portugal annexed to Spain
1583	Expedition by explorer Ralph Fitch

One of the first Englishmen to visit India, Fitch travels around the country for many years.

1588	The defeat of the "undefeatable" Spanish Armada, opens the east to traders other than the Portuguese and the Spanish
1600	Charter for trade given to the English East India Company by Queen Elizabeth I
1602	Founding of the Dutch East India Company
1605	Succession of Akbar's son Jehangir (1592–1666)

Jehangir succeeds in defeating Mewar, and his kingdom extends all over north India except for Orissa.

1608–1649	Tukaram, revered ascetic Marathi poet in the Deccan
1610	Skirmishes between English and Dutch settlers in India
1614	The Danish East India Company founded

1615–1618	Embassy of Sir Thomas Roe at Jehangir's court
1625	Colonial office established in London
1627	Succession of Jehangir's son Shah Jehan (1592–1666)
1627–1680	Sivaji, founder of the Maratha State
1632	Building of the Taj Mahal at Agra

One of the wonders of the world, this marble monument to love will take 20,000 workers (working every day) twenty-two years to build at a cost of 40 million rupees.

1636	Founding of Harvard College in Cambridge, Massachusetts
1639	Settlement of English at Madras

The English set up a factory in Madras in 1641. They buy land, make a fort, and call it Fort St. George.

1645	Building of the Dalai Lama's residence in Lhasa, Tibet

The palace is the official residence of the Dalai Lama, or spiritual head, of Tibetan Buddhists, until 1959, when the present Dalai Lama flees to India with his followers after China's annexation of Tibet.

1650	Arrival of the English at the Hughli River in Bengal

The English take over Portuguese possessions and set up a factory.

1653	Revolt of Sivaji against Bijapur

Sivaji founds a kingdom over vast territory. He is the first Indian leader to talk about Swarajya, *or self-rule.*

1657	Raids on Mughal territories by Sivaji

1658	Shah Jehan imprisoned by his son Aurangzeb (1618 to 1707) who has succeeded to the Mughal throne
1661	Charles II of England betrothed to Catherine of Braganza, whose dowry is Tangier, Bombay, and 300,000 pounds sterling
1664	Founding of French East India Company
1668	Bombay under the control of English East India Company
1669	Religious persecution of Hindus by Aurangzeb
>	Earliest French trading station in India
1670	Continuation of raids against Mughals by Sivaji
1674	Declaration of independence from Aurangzeb by Sivaji Bhonsle, who forms the Maratha state and is crowned at Raigarh
1690	Founding of Calcutta by English colonial administrator, Job Charnock, after defeat of the English East India Company's troops by Aurangzeb's army at Hughli River
1696	Building of Fort William in Calcutta
	By 1701 the English have a governor in Calcutta and supervise local administration.
1698	Founding of the New East India Trading Company in London
	By 1708 the two East India Companies in Britain merge.

1707	Death of Aurangzeb and succession by Bahadur Shah I

Shahuji, Sivaji's grandson, escapes from the Mughal Court and is crowned Chhatrapati, *or King of the Marathas. After the restoration of Shahuji, Marathas are organized by the Peshwa (Prime Minister) Balaji Vishwanath.*

1712	War of Succession between Bahadur Shah I's four sons
1712–1713	Rule of Jahandar Shah, son of Bahadur Shah I, for a year
1713–1719	Rule of Farukh Siyar, son of Bahadur Shah I; control of Farukh by the Sayyid brothers, kingmakers in Delhi
1714	Appointment of the first Peshwa, Balaji Vishwanath of the Bhat family, by Shahuji, grandson of Sivaji, ruler of Satara

This position will become a hereditary Premiership. Under the leadership of the Peshwas the Marathas will gain control or authority over most of northern, central, and southern India. They flourish in the period between the demise of Mughal authority and the establishment of British hegemony in India.

1719	Reign of Mohammed Shah, grandson of Bahadur Shah, who becomes Mughal Emperor, thanks to the good offices of the Sayyid brothers

Muhammed's reign (1719–48) is synonymous with the collapse of Mughal authority. The Mughal territories of Oudh, Orissa, Bihar, and Bengal become virtually sovereign.

1720–1740	Marathas expand under Peshwa Baji Rao, son of Balaji Vishwanath

Marathas are in control over large areas in central and north India and the Deccan. They establish a ferocious reputation.

1722   Austrian East India Company founded

1724   Move of the Mughal Emperor's *wazir*, or minister, Asaf Jah Nizam-ul-Mulk, to Hyderabad; his declaration of independence from Delhi

Asaf Jah, the Mughal authority in the Deccan, founds an independent dynasty far from the "madding crowd" of the decadent Mughal Court in Delhi; this dynasty will last until 1947. His move starts the disintegration of the Mughal Empire for which the coup de grace *would come from yet another plunderer from the north, Nadir Shah.*

1737   Maratha victory over Nizam under Shahuji

1739   Sack of Delhi by Nadir Shah, the ruler of Iran, who massacres 30,000 hapless souls; return of Nadir Shah to Persia carrying a huge booty of cash, valuables, the Peacock Throne, the Koh-i-noor diamond, and the city of Kabul

1740–1761   Period of Anglo-French battle for Indian supremacy; British win after their taking of Arcot, the capital of the Carnatic

1743   Indian yarns imported into Lancashire for manufacture of finer textile goods

The Lancashire textile mills form a powerful lobby which influences the Indian textile industry in a detrimental way.

1745   The creation of Yale University

Yale University is named after Elihu Yale, the benefactor of the Connecticut school from which it is founded. An em-

ployee of the British East India Company, Yale makes his fortune in spices and eventually becomes the Governor of Madras.

1748

French General Joseph Francois Dupleix in control of Carnatic and Hyderabad

In 1749 the Treaty of Aix-la-Chappelle returns Madras to the British.

>

End of Mughal Emperor Mohammed Shah's rule; succession by his son Ahmed Shah

1749

Death of Shahuji, leading to virtual rulership of Marathas by Peshwas

Eventually the Maratha chiefs of the Sindhia, Gaekwad, Bhonsle, and Holkar clans expand independently of each other. After 1772 they no longer operate as a single force under the Peshwa but work as a confederacy under nominal Peshwa leadership.

1751

Succession dispute in Carnatic; annexation of the Carnatic by Robert Clive, an employee of the British East India Company

The French under Dupleix participate in this succession dispute to influence events and establish control. The British are involved, and this develops into a war between the two companies in the guise of support for allies. The capable Dupleix has to give way to Robert Clive who seizes Arcot and the Carnatic in August 1751. Within a decade, the French threat to British power is finished.

1754

End of Mughal Ahmed Shah's rule; succession by Alamgir II with the help of the Marathas and the Nizam

Alamgir II rules for two years and is killed two years after being dethroned by Ahmed Shah Abdali, a general of Nadir

Shah. Abdali proclaims his independence from Nadir Shah and his own suzerainty over Afghanistan. Although the Mughal line is restored in 1771 by the Marathas in the person of Jawan Bakht, son of Shah Alam II (son of Alamgir II), the occupants of the throne are Mughal emperors only in title. The last "Emperor" is Bahadur Shah II whose deportation and death after the Mutiny of 1858 brings to a tragic conclusion the glorious history of the Mughals of India.

1756   Capture of Calcutta by Sirajuddaulah, Nawab of Bengal, to prevent British fortification; infamous "Black Hole of Calcutta" where British men and women die in underground lock-up at Calcutta Fort

1757   Victory for Clive and defeat for Nawab of Bengal in the Battle of Plassey

1758   Clive, Governor of Bengal

1760   The beginning of the Industrial Revolution in Britain

The Industrial Revolution changes European countries, but India remains largely unaffected by its beneficial aspects.

>   Training of Indian armies in European-style tactics and discipline, which continues today

1761   Routing of the Marathas by Afghans under Ahmed Shah Abdali on his fifth invasion of India

>   The British a force in Bengal, Bihar, and Orissa

>   Unsuccessful attack on Poona by the Nizam of Hyderabad

1762   Conquering of Kannara (Mysore) by Hyder Ali Khan (1722–1782), an able and ambitious soldier

1763	Signing of the Treaty of Aurangabad after defeat of Nizam by Marathas at Poona
1764	Occupation of the throne of Mysore by Hyder Ali who becomes a powerful ruler in the south and a serious threat to the British
>	Battle of Buxar between Mir Qasim (and his allies the Mughal Emperor, Shah Alam II, and the Nawab of Oudh) and the British forces ending in Mir Qasim's defeat; establishment of British power over northeastern India

Mir Qasim, the British puppet in Calcutta, has replaced another puppet, Mir Jafar. (Both are bankrupted by corruption in the British East India Company.) Mir Qasim flees Calcutta and returns to be defeated at Buxar. These facts, combined with stories of company servants who flamboyantly enrich themselves by plundering Bengal to the detriment of the Company, provoke Clive's return.

1764–1846	Tyagaraja, one of the greatest composers of Carnatic music
1765	Return of Clive to Calcutta to retake charge following chaos in Bengal

Clive takes the Diwani (revenue title) from the defeated Emperor. This title gives Clive power to collect revenue over a vast area which extends virtually from Bengal and Bihar to central north India.

1770	Devastating famine in Bengal reduces population by one-third; revenue collection by the British continues apace
>	Occupation of Agra and Mathura by the Marathas
1771	Occupation of Delhi by the Marathas and their rein-

stating of the son of Shah Alam II as Mughal Emperor

The Emperor is a puppet of the Marathas. However, the end of the Maratha heyday is approaching as well.

1772   Death of Peshwa Madhav Rao, the great Maratha leader who re-invigorates the Marathas after Abdali; confusion among the disunited Marathas and the beginning of nominal Peshwa rule

1773   Passage of the Regulating Act by Parliament which brings Parliamentary control over the British East India Company

The decadence of the "nabobs" (the term for Indian-made "new rich" British) almost leads the Company to bankruptcy. Inflated dividends (based on inflated assessments of the company's fortunes) are promised to shareholders. As a result, a loan has to be secured from the British government, which also brings the Regulating Act and Parliamentary regulation of the affairs of the Company. The Act brings Madras and Bombay under Calcutta. The Governor is now called the Governor General, and the Governor's Council is now the Governor General's Council. This Council is the parent of the Viceroy's Council of the Act of 1858.

>   Boston Tea Party to protest British taxation on tea

1774   Appointment of Warren Hastings as the Governor General of India with control over Madras, Calcutta, and Bombay

Hastings improves finances for the British East India Company and reforms and expands the existing administrative and judicial infrastructure. He is out of place in a corrupt ethos, but he serves his country well. By diplomacy and military strategy Hastings preserves the gains made on Clive's Diwani.

Hastings is the first governor general to place a British resi-

dent to supervise Company interests in Oudh, which is under the rule of Nawab Shuja-ud-daullah. (Oudh approximates the territories around today's Lucknow in the state of Uttar Pradesh.) The Nawab agrees to pay the Company a subsidy for the "honor" of maintaining its protective troops. This is the cornerstone of the subsidiary system (to be made into a fine art later by Marquis Wellesley) by which the Indian rulers are persuaded to maintain British troops which will eventually take over the very people they are supposed to protect.

> Speech "On American Taxation" by Sir Edmund Burke, conservative British parliamentarian.

> American Revolution

1776 Declaration of Independence by the United States of America

1779 Military and political offensive against the Marathas by Warren Hastings

This British offensive gives impetus to an Indian alliance formed under the famous Nana Phadnavis (advisor to the Peshwa).

1780 Retaliation of Hyder Ali against the Nawab of Arcot for seizure of lands

An alliance consisting of the Marathas, the Nizam, and Hyder Ali threatens British control over the Carnatic. Soon old jealousies and new treachery undermine Indian unity, and the British prosper. Hyder Ali's efforts to unite Indians against the British fall prey to greed and suspicion, and the shaky alliance fails. He is the only member of the alliance not to swerve from his avowed purpose. The alliance defeats the British forces, but in 1782 the Marathas sign the Treaty of Salbai with the British which keeps things under control for the British.

1781	Dutch Settlement in Negapatnam, Madras, captured by the British
1782	Treaty of Salbai between British and Mahadaji Sindhia as a result of the British offensive against the Marathas; Sindhia rises to Maratha forefront
>	Death of Hyder Ali after which his son, Tipu Sultan, takes over and proves himself to be a powerful soldier and leader

The Delhi empire is a caricature of its former self; the north and the south are fragmented; and the country is available to anyone who will manage her fortunes. The success of the British in this task is due, among other things, to unity, superior weaponry, and organization. The Indians, who are divided to start with, have antiquated arms and mercenaries for soldiers.

>	Arrival of Sir William Jones, jurist and scholar, in Calcutta; Jones takes up the study of Sanskrit
1784	Founding of the Asiatic Society of Bengal for the study of Sanskrit by William Jones, resulting in English translations of the *SrimadBhagawadgita, Abhignansakuntalam* and *Ain-i-Akbari*

Three years after his arrival in India, Sir William Jones writes a pioneering paper noting that Greek, Latin, other European languages, and Sanskrit are members of the same language family. 18th century Europe comes to know about the literary heritage of India. This linguistic breakthrough deeply influences Western writers and philosophers.

Jones also introduces the West to ancient Indian legal texts.

>	William Pitts India Act passed by Parliament

The India Act leaves commercial interest to the British East India Company and its ultimate control to the Crown, a dual system which starts the decline of the Company's powers in India. The Act forbids territorial and political expansion as a means to securing good trade, stating that aggression is to be replaced by good government. Needless to say, this is not a profitable idea under the turbulent political conditions prevalent in India where alliances and alignments continue to furnish commercial opportunities for the Company.

> British Peace Treaty at Mangalore with Tipu, Sultan of Mysore, who continues to pursue his anti-British campaigns and soon becomes a legend at home and abroad

1785   Resignation of Hastings after the passage of the Pitts India Act; his return to Britain

1786   Appointment of Lord Cornwallis as the Governor General of India and Commander-in-Chief of the Army

Cornwallis inherits a still-corrupt Company but secures a clean system with strict rules of conduct for the Company employees. He then proceeds to reform and establish an administrative, revenue, and judicial system which endures. He succeeds in redeeming the failing reputation of the Company.

1788   Trial of Warren Hastings for maladministration in India, although he has built upon Clive and strengthened the foundations of the British empire

1789   French Revolution

1790   Policy established under Cornwallis that no Indian is to be employed in a position earning more than 500 pounds a year and that no sepoy (soldier) can rise to commissioned status

Cornwallis' policy is one of many British policies which re-

sult in the humiliation and subjection of India; this particular rule will change only after World War I.

1792   Victory of the British (aided by the Marathas and the Nizam) over Tipu Sultan, ruler of Mysore

Tipu cedes Malabar to the British, which leads to his decline. Like his father, Tipu pleads unsuccessfully for Indian unity.

1793   Establishment by Cornwallis of the Permanent Settlement of Land Revenue in Bengal, which overthrows the traditional relationship between landowner and tenant and makes the British Collector the paramount land revenue authority

The Permanent Settlement of Land Revenue stabilizes revenue by fixing the amount, but it destabilizes the peasant because it does not take the vagaries of nature into consideration. The peasants have only customary rights on the land and are rendered homeless and landless in hard times (which are plentiful). Eventually, many overwhelmed landlords are destroyed as well, while Calcutta city bankers become rich by lending to them. This process gives birth to a new class of Indian, the Western-oriented urban intellectual, who looks to the West for inspiration and prosperity and starts to make the first Indian contacts with British society.

>   Replacement of Cornwallis by Sir John Shore

1794   Death of Mahadaji Sindhia who has established himself as a powerful ruler; this event heralds Maratha collapse

1797–1869   Mirza Asadullah Khan Ghalib, the greatest Urdu poet of all time

Ghalib writes in Persian and Urdu for the Mughal Emperor and for other notables. Still beloved and venerated today, he lives on in the hearts of all lovers of poetry in India.

1798   Appointment of Marquis Wellesley (1760–1842) as
Governor General of India

*When Wellesley takes office, the two remaining threats to the
British are the Marathas and Tipu Sultan. The rest of the
country is in a sad state now. The north and the south is full
of warring chieftains, and the east and other areas are under
the British. The resentment and restlessness of Indians create
British fears of their collusion with a foreign power, such as
Napolean or Russia. Lord Wellesley uses these reasons to
continue imperialism during his term.*

1799   Tipu Sultan killed in battle with the British in
Seringapatam (today's Srirangapatnam); division of
the kingdom of Mysore and its treasures between
Britain and Hyderabad

*Wellesley defeats Tipu at Seringapatam, assisted by his
brother (who the world will remember better as the Duke of
Wellington, hero of Waterloo). More royal families in India
are brought under British control. Wellesley also develops
the Subsidiary System in which the state hands over its protection to the British in return for money (subsidy), thus for-
tifying the state's own potential aggressors. Wellesley breaks
up the Marathas, and in this he is aided by their own dis-
unity.*

1800   Death of Nana Phadnavis, the last great leader of the
Marathas, leaving the Marathas to internal fighting
and decay

>   Machine-made cloth in Britain; leads to the ruination
of Indian handloom and cottage industries

*On the whole, the standard of living of most Indians crashes
and that of the British goes up perceptibly. The indigenous
cotton industry is almost replaced by the British textile industry through any manner found suitable, including, as the
story goes, cutting off the fingers of the weavers of fine
Dhaka muslins. India is now a producer of raw materials for*

British mills, as well as the consumer for the goods manufac-
tured in Britain from these raw materials.

1801   Attack on Poona by Holkar, Maratha ruler of Indore,
        causing Peshwa Baji Rao II to flee to the British side

1802   Signing of the Treaty of Bassein which makes
        Peshwa Baji Rao II a subsidiary of the British

1803   Second Maratha War resulting in the defeat of Sind-
        hia of Gwalior at the hands of the British

        Wellesley collects territories in the Carnatic, the Coastal
        areas, the Deccan, and north India. The Mughal Emperor
        Shah Alam II, following the Marathas and other rulers ac-
        cepts British "protection" as a subsidiary. He is hardly rec-
        ognized even in title by the British.

1804   Outbreak of war between British East India Com-
        pany and Holkar, resulting in the defeat of Holkar's
        army

        The Sikhs emerge now as the only serious challenge to the
        British in India

1805   Recall of Wellesley

        Company Bahadur (Brave) as the British East India Com-
        pany is now called, is in control, but Wellesley has to answer
        to a higher authority, the British Government, and explain
        his unbridled enthusiasm for Indian territory.

1807   Appointment of Lord Minto as the Governor Gen-
        eral of India

1809   Treaty of friendship between Ranjit Singh
        (1780–1839) ruler of the Sikhs, and the British at
        Amritsar whereby it is decided that the British do-

minions will be to the east of the Sutlej River and the Sikh dominions will be to the west

1813   Consolidation of Ranjit Singh's kingdom after he defeats the Afghans at Attock

>   Demonopolization of British East India Company's trade monopoly by the passage of the Parliamentary Charter Act

Now everyone can ply their trade in India. The Charter Act opens the way for missionaries, who come in large numbers from Britain, although smaller numbers have been active in India since 1801. Christian missionaries set up educational institutions.

The British Government asks the Company to set aside 10,000 British pounds for the "English Education" of Indians.

>   British India declared a British Territory

>   Appointment of the Marquess of Hastings as Governor General of India

There is continued widespread terror and lawlessness in India from the Pindaris (unemployed soldiers of erstwhile armies). This problem is addressed by Lord Hastings who removes the scourge.

The British empire is supreme in India. The remaining Indian rulers rule only in name, except for Ranjit Singh of the Sikhs in the Punjab whose power and hegemony continues to rise. By the middle of the nineteenth century, this power also succumbs to the British.

Simla is established as the British summer capital in India.

1815   Reform Movement of Raja Ram Mohan Roy, a Hindu profoundly influenced by Christianity and

Islam, who zealously tries to improve the lot of his countrymen

Raja Ram Mohan Roy incorporates Christian ideals into the formation of the Brahmo Samaj (society) in order to modernize Hinduism and Indian society and thus to reinvigorate young Indians. He translates the Upanishads into modern Bengali for the first time, sets up educational institutions, and tries to synthesize the best of Western and Indian culture.

1817–1898   Sir Syed Ahmed Khan, India's greatest Muslim leader in the 19th century

In 1875 Sir Syed founds the Anglo-Mohammedan Oriental College which will become the Aligarh Muslim University, India's first Western-style Islamic University. Designed after Oxford University, this is one of India's top universities today.

1818   Surrender of Holkar, which along with the later succumbing of Rajasthan, Kathiawar, and central India, completes the consolidation of the British Empire in India

>   First Indian public library in Calcutta

1819   Kashmir added to the Punjab by Ranjit Singh

By 1820 Maharaja Ranjit Singh establishes supreme control over the Punjab and is a force to be reckoned with by the British in terms of power and wealth.

>   The Ajanta caves unearthed

>   Holt Mackenzie's Memorandum which asserts Indian village rights

This Memorandum is in direct contrast to the arbitrary Permanent Settlement of Cornwallis

1823   Discovery of indigenous tea in the Assam hills in the
        northeast of India

1823–1828   Replacement of Hastings by Lord Amherst as Gov-
            ernor General of India

            Amherst (the nephew of the former Governor General of
            Canada from whom he inherits his title) is known in India
            mainly for his Burmese campaign in 1824 as a result of
            which parts of Burma become part of India.

1823–1900   Friedrich Max Mueller, international scholar, linguis-
            tic authority

            Mueller conducts research into the original homeland of the
            Indo-European language family. This quest for a verifiable
            Aryan homeland is still a subject for scholars' discussions.

1828   Reform movement by Raja Ram Mohan Ray to elim-
        inate social evils in India

1828–1835   Appointment of Governor General Lord William
            Bentinck, who makes an impact on some of the pre-
            vailing, if not widespread, social ills of India at the
            time, i.e., *Sati*, or self-immolation by widows, and in-
            fanticide

            Sati, the practice of a widow's immolating herself on her
            husband's funeral pyre, is not universally practiced, but ex-
            ists in pockets, where a widow is forced into it by her in-
            law's greed for inheritance or by a family's intolerance of
            dependent widows or by religious fanaticism.

1829   Abolishing of *Sati* in British India

1829–1912   Allen Octavian Hume, member of the Theosophical
            Society, and moving spirit behind the Indian Na-
            tional Congress, India's largest political party

1830   Addition of Mysore to British possessions

>   Indians taken as indentured laborers to other British colonies

This practice will take millions of Indians abroad over the next century. Among the descendents of these Indians are the eminent writer V. S. Naipaul (West Indies), President Cheddi Jagan (Guyana), and professional golfer Vijay Singh (Fiji Islands)

1833   Passage of the Charter Act under which British East India Company is now simply deputizing as a trustee for the Crown in India; inclusion in the Act of a declaration of equality for all before the law, at least in theory

The Parliament takes over the Company's possessions, and a Law Commission is established to codify the judicial system. This results later in the creation of the Indian Evidence Act, Indian Penal Code, the Civil Code, and other legal codes which are basically still the backbone of the courts in India. The Act adds a Law Member to the Governor General-in-Council, and this body can now pass legislative acts for British India. Lord Macaulay joins Bentinck as the first Law Member of the Governor General's Council in Calcutta. He suggests education reforms and decides to create a class of Indians educated in the English style so as to provide auxiliary staff for the Company.

1834   Formation of Committee under Bentinck to initiate tea cultivation in India

1835   Declaration of English as the official language replacing Persian after half a millennium

1836   Appointment of Lord Auckland, Governor General of India

1837	Deciphering of Asoka's edicts by James Prinsep
1838	Tripartite Treaty between Ranjit Singh, the deposed Shah Shuja of Afghanistan, and the British after the First Afghan War

The treaty is designed to restore Shuja and to establish the British presence in Afghanistan in the wake of rumors of a Russian invasion.

1839	Death of Ranjit Singh, founder of Sikh Kingdom; subsequent decline of his autocratic political system
1839–1842	First Opium War between Britain and China

The Chinese try to prevent the British from illegally selling opium to the Chinese who have become addicted in large numbers to the drug. However, the Chinese lose, and by the end of the Opium Wars the British acquire Hong Kong as well unrestricted rights to sell Indian opium in China.

1844	Succession struggles among Ranjit Singh's chieftains making them susceptible to manipulation by the British
1845	Onset of Anglo-Sikh War
1845–49	British conquest of the Punjab and Kashmir
1846	Defeat of the Sikhs by the British
1848	Revolt of the Sikhs; beginning of the second Sikh War
1848–56	Appointment of Lord Dalhousie as Governor General of India; completion of the suzerainty of the British

Dalhousie firmly believes in the superiority of the British race over the Indians and thus appoints himself to "civilize" the natives. His stewardship sees many educational and social reforms designed to enable the natives to benefit from "superior" Western enhancements; there is a proliferation of British-style colleges and grants-in-aid in India. Among Dalhousie's other reforms is one which allows Christian converts to inherit their Hindu property. He also formulates the highly profitable (to the British) Doctrine of Lapse, whereby native territories lapse to the British in the absence of natural heirs to the ruler. Dalhousie annexes the Punjab and other Indian states on charges of misgovernment, and he abolishes the titles of the native rulers. The telegraph and railways are introduced to India.

1849   The defeat of the Sikhs and their surrender at Rawalpindi

The British finally win the Punjab and sign a treaty with the Maharajah at Lahore. They take Kashmir, which is later sold to Ghulab Singh, the helpful Chieftain of Jammu. The Punjab (Punj: Five, Ab: Water, i.e., the land of five rivers, the Indus, Sutlej, Beas, Ravi, and Chenab) continues its tradition of feeding Indians and the British from its well-irrigated and prosperous agricultural countryside.

1853   Passage of the Charter Act which removes the last vestige of Company power and introduces competitive examinations for selection to the Indian Civil Service

The selection to the Indian Civil Service is now to be made through an open examination instead of through personal appointment. The post-independence Indian Administrative Service is patterned to a very large extent on the (British) Indian Civil Service in terms of recruitment and organization.

>   First railway (Great Indian Peninsular Railway) and telegraph system established in India

> Visit of Sir Alexander Cunningham to the Harappa site

Cunningham is intrigued by the huge mounds of earth that he finds at Harappa. Twenty years later he visits Harappa several times again and finds several seals, fired bricks, and other objects, which eventually lead to the amazing discovery of the Indus Valley Civilization.

> The Madras Native Association formed among the upper classes

1854 Passage of the Assam Clearance Act which gives away land to European planters who will plant tea

The difficulties encountered with Chinese tea are salvaged by the momentous discovery of indigenous Indian tea. With their usual resourcefulness, the British put this discovery to use in short order. Eventually, Indian tea replaces Chinese tea in world trade although not one Indian owns a tea estate.

> Beginnings of a Legislative Council in Calcutta

1855 Postal and telegraph systems combined in India

> Establishment of the first Indian industrial business by Dadabhai Naoroji, a Parsi intellectual, nationalist, and critic of the British effect on the economy of India

Later Naoroji, called the "Grand Old Man" of Indian politics, will be the first Indian elected to the British Parliament in 1892. As three-time President of the Indian National Congress, he is a catalyst and orator for the freedom movement.

1856 Annexation of Oudh by the British, devastating the ruler, who feels betrayed and humiliated, a feeling shared now by the rank and file in India

1856–1862   Appointment of Lord Canning as India's last governor general and then first viceroy

Canning enacts a law permitting Hindu widows to remarry. He is comparatively sympathetic to Indians, an attitude quite out of keeping with the times.

1856–1920   Bal Gangadhar Tilak, revolutionary nationalist leader

Tilak relies on Maratha and Hindu traditions for inspiration and calls on his compatriots to reject British ways and ideas.

1857   Indian Mutiny, or Revolt, or first and last War of Independence, at Meerut

\>   Opening of three Presidency universities in Madras, Bombay, and Calcutta

1858   Passage of Government of India Act by the British Parliament after the proclamation of British victory over the Mutiny

The Act completes the transfer of full powers from the British East India Company to the Crown. It appoints a Secretary of State for India, who has full power and responsibility for India and who is a member of the British Cabinet. He is to be aided by a Council of India (at Whitehall, site of the British Government in London) of fifteen members, seven of whom will be from the East India Company. However, the actual governmental control in India is with the Governor General in India (now called Viceroy), his Council, and the large bureaucracy called the Indian Civil Service which is posted in the "field" throughout the country. The governmental structure of India is gradually becoming defined.

The Proclamation of Queen Victoria rejects the Doctrine of Lapse and upholds treaties with zamindars (or landlords) perceived to be loyal during the revolt. Lord Canning holds the Lucknow Durbar at which land titles are given out to the faithful wealthy; the latter are eager for the honors and quite unmindful of their subjection.

1859   Complete control of the British established over the Indian subcontinent

The cost of the mutiny is charged to India, which pays it off in the next four years by increasing government revenue. This revenue comes from agriculture, the illicit opium trade with China, salt tax, customs duty, and income tax.

1859–1860   "Blue Mutiny" or the first labor strike organized by Indians against British management

The "Blue Mutiny" is provoked by the inhuman working conditions of the indigo laborers. Indigo has been exported from India to Europe from the twelfth century, and its export continues until the manufacture of synthetic dyes in Europe at the end of the nineteenth century.

1860   Introduction of coffee in south India; not a successful venture as the crop is susceptible to disease

>   The commencement of the Indian Railway system

1861   Passage of the Indian Councils Act and the introduction of Provincial Legislative Councils in Bombay, Madras, and Bengal

These Councils are appointed by the powers that be; there is no electorate or representation. The members of the Viceroy's Executive Council oversee departments for which they are responsible. The membership of the Executive Council is increased, and at least half are non-official. The non-officials are Indians appointed by the British. This Executive Council is located in Calcutta. The Provincial Legislative Councils are located in Bombay, Madras, and Calcutta.

>   Creation of the Order of the Star of India by Queen Victoria

1861–86   American Civil War

1861–1941	Rabindranath Tagore, patriot, philosopher, artist, poet and Nobel laureate
1862–63	Appointment of Lord Elgin, eighth earl, Viceroy, in India
1864	Selection of Satyendranath Tagore as the first Indian to enter the Indian Civil Service
1864–69	Appointment of Lord John Lawrence as Viceroy
1865–1928	Lala Lajpat Rai, nationalist and moving spirit behind the spread of the reformist movement of Arya Samaj (society)

The Arya Samaj emphasizes the "fundamental" Vedas and is alive and well in north India today.

1865–1936	Indian-born Rudyard Kipling, author of *Kim* and *Jungle Book* and several other British stories on India; Nobel Prize winner
1866–1915	Gopal Krishna Gokhale, moderate reformer and national leader
1869–1948	Mohandas Karamchand Gandhi, the Father of the Indian Nation
1869	Completion of the Suez Canal

With the completion of the Suez Canal and the introduction of the steamship, the sea passage to India is shortened dramatically. British officers begin to go home for vacations, rather than touring India and understanding her as their predecessors had done. Thus, India becomes a tour-of-duty, rather than a vocation.

>	Appointment of Lord Mayo as Viceroy

1870	Poona Sarvajanik Sabha (Social Welfare Society) founded by Mahadev Govind Ranade
>	Tea in the Nilgiri Hills of Tamil Nadu
1872–1876	Appointment of Lord Northbrook as Viceroy after Mayo's assassination in the Andaman Islands
1873	Several tea estates in Darjeeling

Darjeeling tea, universally regarded as high quality tea, continues to be India's preeminent tea export today.

>	British East India Company no longer in existence
1873–1962	Fazlul Haq, President of the Muslim League and Bengali leader; first Prime Minister of East Bengal
1875	Founding of Theosophical Society by Madame Blavatsky in New York after which she sets up her own *Samaj,* or Society, in Adyar
>	Founding of the Arya Samaj by Swami Dayananda Saraswati, who believes in reforming and simplifying Hinduism by returning to the pristine religion followed by Vedic Aryans
1875–1950	Sardar Vallabhai Patel, nationalist leader and India's first Deputy Prime Minister
1876–80	Appointment of Lord Lytton as Viceroy
1876	Founding of the Indian Association, India's first nationalist political organization, by Surendranath Bannerjea (1848–1925), national leader, after he is unfairly dismissed from the prestigious Indian Civil

Service to which he had been selected in a rigorous competitive examination

Bannerjea, like other contemporary Indian leaders (Gokhale, Tilak, Ranade, and others) is a professor, newspaper editor, and patriot.

1876–1949   M. A. Jinnah, *Quaid-i-Azam* of Pakistan; the creator of Pakistan

Jinnah is a brilliant lawyer with a thriving practice, and an active participant in the Congress national movement. Jinnah then becomes the preeminent Muslim national leader in pre-independence India. Given the honorific Quaid-i-Azam (Great Leader), Jinnah is the main architect, leader, and mentor behind the Muslim League and the birth of Pakistan. He becomes the Chief Executive or Governor General of Pakistan after independence.

1876   Queen Victoria, Empress of India

It is reported that she takes Hindi lessons.

>   Famine in Bengal

1877–1938   Sir Muhammed Iqbal, intellectual, poet-philosopher, and mentor of Pakistan

1879   Massacre of British troops at the Khyber Pass after the Afghan War

>   Removal of duties on Lancashire cotton and imposition of heavy excise duties on Indian cotton

1879–1949   Sarojini Naidu, "Nightingale of India;" feminist; freedom fighter; first Indian woman President of the Indian National Congress; first woman Governor of an Indian State

1880–1884	Appointment of Lord Ripon as Viceroy

Ripon is liked throughout India and is remembered as the first Viceroy to sincerely, but unsuccessfully, attempt to install democratic processes in British India, starting at the municipal and district levels.

1882	Jute industry in full force in Bengal

1883	Convening of the first Indian National Congress by Surendranath Bannerjea, who eventually serves as its president

1884–88	Appointment of Lord Dufferin as Viceroy

1885	Annexation of Burma by British troops sent by Dufferin

>	First meeting of the Indian National Congress under Womesh C. Bonnerjea in Bombay

Allen Octavian Hume (who is considered to be the father of the Indian National Congress), William Wedderburn, and other Englishmen attend the meeting. Womesh C. Bonnerjee, a Calcutta barrister, presides over the gathering of whom most are Hindus from an emerging educated middle class. Although the Congress at this stage is very loyal to the Crown and hopes through this forum to bring the attention of the Crown to its grievances, it is looked down upon as inconsequential by most Britishers.

1887–1920	Srinivasa Ramanujan, self-taught mathematician and pioneer in mathematical discoveries

A man of few means, Ramanujan has to take a petty job to make ends meet. Working on mathematics in his spare time, he goes beyond all his contemporaries, thus stirring the curiosity of British mathematicians who help him come to Britain. Two years before his untimely death he is selected as the first Indian in the Royal Society of London. At his death, he is recognized by his peers as an unrivaled genius; mathe-maticians today are still at work on his theorems.

1887–1958 Maulana Abul Kalam Azad, national freedom movement leader, Congress President, and India's first Minister for Education

1888–94 Appointment of Lord Landsdowne as Viceroy

1889–1964 Pandit Jawaharlal Nehru, national leader and first Prime Minister of India after independence

1890–1988 Khan Abdul Ghaffar Khan, leader of the Northwest Frontier Province and the Pathans

Khan Sahib is called the "Frontier Gandhi" because he is a disciple of the Mahatma.

1891–1956 Dr. Bhimrao Ramji Ambedkar, intellectual, nationalist, and leader of his community, the "untouchables"

The "untouchables" are renamed Harijan (or God's People) by Mahatma Gandhi with whom Ambedkar works to change the rigid attitudes of casteism. Ambedkar is one of the framers of the Constitution of India and becomes India's Law Minister in 1947. However, he turns to Buddhism in the end because he is disillusioned by the persistence of caste prejudice in India.

1892 Indian Councils Act of 1892: addition of members to the Legislative Council

The constitutional structure becomes a little enlarged. Members of the Central Legislative Council are still nominated by the viceroy though they are selected now from submitted lists of members of various public bodies. The Council Act also expands membership in the Viceroy's Council. The expanded Viceroy's council has 16 members of whom 10 are non-official members. They can ask questions and criticize the official budget one day in each year, there still is no representa-

tion or direct election. The British officials still run the show, and the Indians want much more.

1893	Revival of the Ganapati Festival by Tilak, who also publishes the *Kesari* newspaper in Marathi in order to reach the common man
>	Gandhi at Durban in South Africa as legal counselor
>	Aurobindo Ghosh's advocation of action (rather than moderation) in the quest for freedom
>	Annie Besant, Director of the Theosophical Society in Adyar
>	Lord Landsdowne's demarcation of the Durand line, which delineates Indo-Afghan borders

Lord Elgin and Lord Curzon try unsuccessfully to subjugate the warlike people of Afghanistan.

1893–1963	Husein Shaeed Suhrawardy, Muslim League Leader; later Prime Minister of Pakistan
1894–98	Appointment of Lord Elgin, ninth earl, as Viceroy
1895	Sivaji festivals started by Tilak, who moves India with the cry, "Swarajya is my birthright and I will have it*!*"
1896–1951	Liaquat Ali Khan, Muslim leader, member of the first Interim Government of India; first Prime Minister of Pakistan
1897	Severe famine, plague, and economic depression in India

The turn of the century is dismal for India.

> Queen Victoria's Diamond Jubilee

> Assassination of two British officers by young Indian nationalists after Jubilee celebration

> Founding of Indian National Social Conference by Ranade, an Indian nationalist, with the aim of implementing social reform neglected by the British

The National Social Conference eventually merges with the Indian National Congress.

As far as Indian social issues are concerned, the British believe in letting things go, no matter how undesirable they are in the Western context, so as not to rouse Indian fears and suspicions. The attempt to reform India's social ills falls into the hands of patriotic Indians who want their homeland to improve in every way.

1897–1945 Subhash Chandra Bose, freedom fighter

1899–1905 Appointment of Lord Curzon as Viceroy

1900 Production by India of over four hundred million pounds of cotton yarn

> Displacement of China as a leading tea producer by India; India exports over six million pounds of tea; displacement of India by China as opium producer

1901 Founding of Vishwa Bharati University at Santiniketan by Tagore; the University exemplifies Tagore's ideas and becomes one of India's most prestigious universities

> Creation by Lord Curzon of the Northwest Frontier

Province on the Indo-Afghan border to reduce border conflicts with Afghan tribes

1903   Coronation Durbar for Edward VI, King Emperor at Delhi

1904   Conquest of Tibet by Colonel Younghusband

1905   Curzon's partitioning of Bengal

Curzon's partition leads to a political upheaval with long term consequence as it provokes the first mass agitation in India and provides a rallying point for disparate Indian leaders. He has earlier created the Northwest Frontier Province to deal with the Afghan border problem. Neither of these acts brings the desired results, i.e., interior and exterior calm. A capable but shortsighted administrator, Lord Curzon resigns and leaves India.

>   Appointment of Earl of Minto as Viceroy

1906   Demand for *Swarajya* by Dadabhai Naoroji in Bombay

>   Entrance of Muhammed Ali Jinnah into politics when he becomes Dadabhai Naoroji's political secretary

>   Founding of the All-India Muslim League by the Aga Khan (the leader of the Ismailis, a Muslim sect)

Aga Khan III and Muslim leaders meet Viceroy Minto in Simla and ask him to safeguard Muslim interests by ensuring their representation on official councils; the Viceroy is sympathetic to their cause and assures them of separate electorates. The Muslim League is then organized to protect Indian Muslims, to support and approve partition, and to show loyalty to the sympathetic British government. The League holds its first meeting in Dhaka, but at this stage it represents only a select group of Muslims.

> Victory of the Liberal party in Britain, which marks openness and new reforms for India

John Morley, Secretary of State for India at Whitehall, and Viceroy Minto jointly write the Morley-Minto Reforms. The Reforms are the basis for the Indian Councils Act of 1909, providing for direct elections, an important advance in the constitutional development of India. Morley rejects British opposition and accepts advice from Gokhale and other Indian leaders.

> Start of a new newspaper, *Bande Matram*, which extols the Boycott as an indispensable tool in the freedom movement started by Bipin Chandra Pal and Aurobindo Ghosh, radical leaders

The Boycott movement, named after an Irish patriot, calls for Indians to have nothing to do with British goods. Initially it leads to bonfires of British textiles and the use of Indian handloom cloth called Swadeshi *(from our land), and it soon spreads to self-reliance in all areas, giving economic fuel to the nationalist movement.*

1907   Split of the Indian National Congress on the issue of extremism, a split which will last for nine years

There is much debate at this time about radical vs. moderate means to achieve the same end, freedom, and the two dissenting groups are named Moderates and Extremists.

The British government cracks down on nationalist disturbances, and mass arrests follow as does severe oppression for the Indians. Tilak is imprisoned in Mandalay for six years.

> Anglo-Russian Convention, which delineates the spheres of influence of these two major powers

*Afghanistan remains largely under British hands until the
Treaty following the Third Afghan War, which assures
Afghanistan's external and internal independence. History
has shown the Afghans to be an intrepid nation to this day.
Rudyard Kipling's story* The Man who would be King *seems
to be a fictionalized account of British misadventures in
Afghanistan.*

> Founding of Tata Iron and Steel by Jamshed N.
Tata, India's great industrialist

*The Tatas are among India's preeminent industrialists even
today.*

1908　Terrorism on the rise in India

> Call for open revolution in terrorist paper *Yugantar*

> Recognition af Aga Khan as Honorary Permanent
President of the Muslim League for his support of
the League

1909　Passage of the Indian Councils Act based on the
Morley-Minto Reforms

*A huge step in the constitutional evolution of India, Morley's
main contribution to constitutional reform is direct elections
to Indian legislative bodies as well as their expansion in
membership. Now, there are Indians in the Council of India
at Whitehall, the Viceroy's Executive Council, the Imperial
Legislative Assembly, and the provincial legislatures, fulfilling some of the promise of equality for Indians given earlier.
The Act also increases the number of members of the
Supreme Legislative Council and the provincial legislative
councils, and it abolishes official majorities in the provincial
legislatures. Elections are introduced for the first time, even
if they are not based on Universal Adult Suffrage. The
Viceroy retains the power of veto.*

Morley sets great store by the great British institution of par-

liamentary government; thus, he overrides Raj skepticism and introduces the beginnings of parliamentary procedure such as questions, debates, and introduction of legislative proposals throughout India. In 1909 these are brave moves to make, but they do not keep pace with the expectations created by the rapidly rising national movement.

Separate Muslim Electorates are also introduced by the Viceroy's orders, a result of the 1906 meeting.

> Appointment of Sir S. P. Sinha, Advocate-General of Bengal, as the first Indian Law Member of the Viceroy's Executive Council

> Assassination of British assistant to John Morley by an Indian in London

This act of violence leads to the imprisonment of hundreds of radical nationalists. Veer Savarkar, a young radical, is deported to the Andaman Islands, a popular place for exile. The islands are called Kala Pani *("black water") in Hindi, no doubt because the waters surrounding them are virtually impassable.*

1910   Appointment of Lord Hardinge, Liberal, as Viceroy

> Escape of Sri Aurobindo, revolutionary mentor of young nationalists, to French Pondicherry where he founds the Aurobindo Ashram with a French mystic, universally called the "Mother"

I met this mystical lady while I was on tour as a young officer in the Indian Administrative Service.

1911   Iron and steel production in Jamshedpur

> Coronation Durbar of King George V at Delhi in which both the King and Queen are present

At the Durbar the reunification of Bengal is announced. The shifting of the Government's capital to New Delhi is also announced. The new capital will be built in a city which has been a capital to many rulers. Designed by Sir Edward Lutyens and Sir Herbert Baker, Delhi will architecturally represent the glory of the Imperial Raj.

1912	Wounding of Viceroy Hardinge in a bomb attack
1913	Muslim League Party joined by Jinnah
>	Formation of the Ghadar, or (Revolutionary) Mutiny Party, in the United States by the Punjabis, most of whom are Sikhs
>	Arrest in South Africa of Gandhi, leader of Passive Resistance Movement
>	Awarding of the Nobel Prize for Literature to Rabindranath Tagore
1914	Declaration of war against Germany by Great Britain; the onset of World War I ; total support of Britain's war effort by all parts and parties of India; hope created that Indian support will bring India independence in exchange
>	Sikhs, intending to migrate to Canada, sent back to Calcutta on Japanese ship after they are refused admittance in Vancouver, Canada
>	Founding of the Hindu Mahasabha, a Hindu party, by Pandit Madan Mohan Malaviya (1861–1946)
>	Dravida Kazhagam, anti-Aryan and anti-priestly-class organization,formed by E. V. Ramaswami Naicker, popularly called *Periyar,* or Great Leader

The Dravida Kazhagam will be the springboard in 1949 for the Dravida Munetra Kazhagam organized by C. N. Annadurai. Today the D.M.K. continues to play a powerful and key role in the politics of Tamil Nadu, representing a broad-based constituency.

1915   Return to India of Gandhi who joins the freedom movement

1916   Temporary unity between different factions brought about by the Lucknow Pact

The Congress and the League seek election and other administrative reforms. Congress agrees to accommodate the Muslims with more seats in all the legislative councils, thus laying the foundations for working with the League for the common goal of attaining independence from the British. This camaraderie does not last very long.

1916–1921   Appointment of Lord Chelmsford as Viceroy

>   Formation of an Industrial Board to survey India's industrial potential

>   Death of thousands of Indian soldiers in the war not only from enemy fire, but from inadequate supplies as well

The bravery shown and the heavy casualties suffered by Indian soldiers belie the British prejudice; Indians are now allowed into the officer's ranks as Royal Commissioned Officers, a rank that has been denied them since 1790. This change does not truly affect the officers or the other ranks because they soon suffer a relapse from their brief glory of war heroism to the indignity of being Indian under the British Raj.

Edwin Samuel Montagu, a Liberal, becomes the Secretary of State. He makes a plea for progress in political participation for Indians, and this effort intensifies after the contribution

*made by India to the World War I effort. Britain is only now
beginning to sense the momentum of the national movement.*

1917   Annie Besant, President of the Indian National Congress, the only British woman ever to hold the post

>   The Bolshevik (Russian) Revolution

>   Procuration of war materials from India for Allies expedited by Munitions Board

>   Proclamation in the House of Commons of the British Parliament promising gradual progress towards responsible government and self- rule for India after World War I

>   Aid and support for the indigo workers and peasants by Gandhi

1918   "Report on Indian Constitutional Reform" by Montagu, calling for Dyarchy which is seen as a *via media* between British control and Indian Self Rule

*The policy of Dyarchy divides the functions of government
into those reserved for the appointed officers and those
transferred to elected representatives. Gandhi rejects the
principle of dyarchy as being an insufficient response to Indian demands.*

1919   Passage of Rowlatt Acts, which perpetuate wartime rules pertaining to freedom of speech and expression, thus exposing the insincerity of the British towards the Indians who have fought loyally on their side

*Gandhi rallies the country to civil disobedience against the
Acts, advising Indians to practice a general boycott rejecting
British services and institutions. He is arrested by the man*

who will shortly thereafter hasten the demise of the British Empire in India, i.e., General R.E.H. Dyer. The Jallianwalla Bagh Massacre (at which thousands of Indians at a gathering in a public park are killed by gunfire under Dyer's orders) sends the country into shock. Lord Chelmsford tries to cover up the tragedy, but Montagu asks for an inquiry into the details. Dyer is relieved of his command and returns to Britain, where he is presented with a collected purse of thousands of pounds.

> Passage of the Government of India Act based on the Montagu-Chelmsford Reforms

This Act, which defines the Government of India still further, installs Dyarchy between Indian representatives and Crown officials, increases the number of Indians in the Viceroy's Executive Council, and makes the Supreme Legislative Council into a bicameral legislature, i.e., the Imperial Legislature and the Council of State. The number of enfranchised Indians to all legislatures is increased, and the electorate for the provincial legislature now numbers around five million although not based on Universal Adult Suffrage. It is proposed that Dyarchy wil be reviewed after ten years.

> Third Afghan War

1919–1930 Jinnah, President of the Muslim League

1920 First meeting of the All-India Trade Union Congress under the leadership of Lala Lajpat Rai

The trade union movement starts in India, aided by the mobilization of mass support by Gandhi. Today, one in four Indian workers is a union member, and there are several trade unions.

> The beginnings of the Communist Party of India

> Summary of India's contribution to the war effort includes deployment of a million Indian soldiers, the

loss of tens of thousands of lives, thousands of injuries, military goods worth hundreds of millions of British pounds, wheat, raw jute and jute sacks, and cash for wartime expenditures

> Gandhi's non-cooperation movement

A part of this non-cooperation movement is cooperation with the Khilafat movement, which protests the British alliance with Greece against the Caliph of Turkey. The Caliph is regarded by the Muslims as their spiritual leader, and the Khilafat movement calls for his restoration. At this point the non-cooperation movement is in full force, and even the visit of the Prince of Wales does not dampen its ardor.

Gandhi advocates boycott of elections, but the more moderate members of Congress participate in them.

1921 Harappa excavations under Sir John Marshall; Mohenjo Daro discovered by R. D. Bannerjee

> Elections based on the Government of India Act of 1919

> Anglo-Afghan Treaty assuring mutual independence of the two countries

> Separation of Hindus and Muslims in their quest for freedom and acceleration of incidents of violence between them

Gandhi emphasizes mass civil disobedience, but he is soon to realize that not everyone can carry that torch safely.

> Appointment of Lord Reading as Viceroy

1922 Gandhi's plan for disobedience in Bardoli (near Bombay) abandoned when he hears of violence at Chauri Chaura (in the United Provinces)

Instead of activism, Gandhi takes up weaving khadi, *or homespun cloth, and asks Indians to prepare themselves by learning self-control in order to avoid violence. Gandhi is imprisoned and released two years later . This signals a temporary halt to civil disobedience.*

>   Abstention from political agitation by Gandhi; new Congress leadership under Motilal Nehru and C.R. Das, which will last for the next seven years

1923   Lord Reading's attempts to win Indian support by measures such as holding Indian Civil Service examinations in New Delhi as well as in London and admitting Indians to the Military Academy for officer training

                Lord Reading is sympathetic to the reform demands of Indian liberals, and he also abolishes the cotton tax although the salt tax is increased to make up for the loss of revenue

1924   Release of Gandhi after he fasts for 21 days against the religious feuds (called communalism in India) of Hindus and Muslims

1925   Congress dues now to be paid in *khadi*

                Gandhi feels that this measure will make the elitist Congress leadership more in touch with the masses. The khadi *can be woven by anyone, and the theme of "homespun" captures the nation.*

1926–1931   Appointment of Lord Irwin as Viceroy

1927   Review of Dyarchy and constitutional reforms proposed by the Simon Commission; no self-rule in sight for Indians yet; rejection of the Commission by all Indians, whether of the Congress, League, or other persuasion

After the departure of the Simon Commission, Motilal Nehru draws up a draft Constitution for India. The draft proposal causes representational anxiety in the League camp.

1929 Beginning of the Great Depression in the United States of America and Europe, set off by the crash of the stock market in the U.S.

> Lahore Congress persuaded by Jawaharlal Nehru and Subhash Chandra Bose to accept only *Purna Swarajya*, or complete independence

After the failure of the Simon Commission causes increasing suspicion about British motives, young leaders such as Nehru and Bose reject the dominion status promised by the British.

1930 A declaration of Independence, or *Purna Swarajya*, in Lahore on January 26th

This is celebrated as Republic Day in India today.

> Nobel Prize for Physics awarded to Sir C. V. Raman

> Convening of the First Round Table Conference in London

British political party representatives and Indian community representatives are present with the exception of the Congress. Nothing is achieved except a glamorous gathering of princes and other notables.

> Breaking of the salt law by Gandhi who picks up British-owned salt (found on Indian seashores) after which he is hailed for this violation of the law by poetess Sarojini Naidu (a devoted freedom fighter); mass arrests of many Congress workers and leaders

> Sir Muhammed Iqbal's proposal at the annual con-

ference of the League at Allahabad to create a Muslim State as the final destiny of Muslims

Sir Mohammad Iqbal, an intellectual, poet, and President of the Muslim League, lists the areas which should comprise the state of Pakistan, i.e., Punjab, Sindh, Baluchistan, and the North West Frontier Province. In Cambridge, Britain, three years later the name Pakistan is devised by Rahmat Ali from the five areas or peoples envisaged as a part of Pakistan (i.e., Punjab, Afghan, Kashmir, and Sindh). Bengal does not seem to figure in these calculations yet.

1931   Release of Gandhi by Lord Irwin

Irwin has talks with Gandhi which result in the Gandhi-Irwin Pact, assuring Government approval of the Swadeshi movement, but not of the Boycott. Gandhi calls off the civil disobedience agitation in return for the release of non-violent prisoners. This is regarded as "giving in to the enemy" by some of the leaders.

>   Second Round Table Conference

The Muslims, the Sikhs, and the Depressed Classes ("untouchables") all demand separate electorates; Gandhi will not agree to it, but is ignored. Gandhi's demand for self-rule is also ignored; he returns, disillusioned, to India and resumes political agitation. He is arrested, and the Third Round Table Conference is held without him.

1931–34   Jinnah practicing law in London

1931–36   Appointment of Lord Willingdon as Viceroy

1932   Founding of the All-Jammu and Kashmir Muslim Conference by Sheikh Mohammed Abdullah

This party will later be named the National Conference to reflect the secular nature of the organization.

>   Announcement of the Communal Award by Ramsey

MacDonald, Prime Minister of Britain, giving separate electorates to anyone who will ask for them

This Award is deeply resented by Congress and Gandhi in particular. He meets Ambedkar, the leader of the "untouchables", and concludes the Yeravada Pact. As a result, untouchability is denounced, and the Award fails to partition the Hindu community.

> Discovery of Indus seals at the Sumerian archaeological excavations at Ur

> Third Round Table Conference

This Conference leads to the Government of India Act of 1935.

1933 The release due to lack of evidence of the suspected members of a communist conspiracy in Meerut

Jawaharlal Nehru takes up the cause of the suspects, thus rallying the youth and labor movements behind him. Nehru is chosen by Gandhi as the next leader for the Congress over Subhash Chandra Bose, an immensely popular freedom fighter known as Netaji *or "respected leader."*

1934 Return of Jinnah from London

Jinnah starts work on revitalizing the Muslim League, looks for grassroots support for what has so far been only an elitist organization.

1935 Passage of the Government of India Act, longest statute ever to be framed by the British Parliament and the beginning of the process of handing over power to India

A major step towards defining the constitution of India is taken when the Government of India Act is drafted by Sir Samuel Hoare. The Act provides for provincial autonomy, which is incorporated for the first time into the British-made

*Indian Constitution and is inaugurated two years later after
nationwide elections. The Act provides for a federation at the
center of British India, this is not implemented. (Later, the
Indian constitution will create a federation.) Now India has
a Supreme Court but the Viceroy retains special authority.
The Electorate, though still restricted, now numbers about
40 million, and separate electorates are retained. Elections
are held, and the Congress emerges triumphant, if not completely satisfied. This is the first time that the Indians are
participating in the government with the British. However,
since the Act falls short of* Purna Swarajya, *it is regarded as
an extension of the subjection of India.*

*The framers of the constitution of independent India will use
parts of this Act as a starting point.*

1936 Victory of Congress by an absolute majority in the
first elections under the new constitution

*After vacillating, the Congress takes office as a means to an
end.*

*The Muslim League fares badly in the elections, and its elit-
ist nature and internal dissensions are blamed for the disappointment. Therefore, Jinnah tries to win over Fazlul Haq of
the Krishi Praja Party and Sir Sikander Hyat Khan and his
Unionist party, as well as others, since these parties have a
strong following in the rural areas. Jinnah then announces
that Muslims all over India have been organized and are
now united in their demands, and hence only the Muslim
League can represent India's Muslims. Nehru disagrees.
Meetings with top Congress leaders fail, and the rift between
the Congress and the League deepens further*

> Appointment of Lord Linlithgow as Viceroy

1939 Break between Netaji Subhash Chandra Bose and
Congress; formation of his own party, which is called
the Forward Bloc

> Announcement by Lord Linlithgow that India, along

with Britain, is at war with Germany, causing a shock among Indians who felt their permission was not requested; resignation of Congress ministries

> Proclamation by Jinnah that Friday, December 22 is Muslim India's Deliverance Day from Congress's tyranny

1940   Lahore meeting of Muslim League calling for the creation of a separate Muslim state; several proposals as to how this can be accomplished

This meeting results in the Lahore (commonly called the Pakistan) Resolution. Jinnah emphasizes separateness. Gandhi reiterates his stand on the common background (since antiquity) of all Indians.

> Linlithgow's invitation to Simla extended to all Indian leaders; offer to create the War Advisory Council

Linlithgow's offer is designed to soothe the indignation the Indian leaders have felt at not being involved in the Declaration of War. Jinnah meets with Linlithgow and assures him of support; in turn, Linlithgow assures Jinnah of Muslim participation in all future steps towards the constitutional development of India.

> Satyagraha launched by Gandhi to protest war effort in a non-violent way; mass arrests

1941   Flight of Bose to Berlin where he is welcomed by Hitler

Bose broadcasts to his followers in India and urges them to revolt against their oppressors.

> Signing of Atlantic Charter by Churchill and Roosevelt affirming basic principles of the Rights of Man

Churchill declares that this Charter does not apply to Indians, Burmese, and some other subjects of the British empire.

> Japanese attack on Pearl Harbor and other possessions of the Allied Forces

1942 Singapore taken by Japanese who provide Bose with 60,000 soldiers (newly released Indian POW"s) for his Indian National Army; Japan on the threshold of eastern India

> Reluctant Churchill persuaded to send the Cripps Mission to India to resolve the political deadlock; failure of the mission

The immediate departure of the British (in order to avoid the imminent Japanese threat) is now demanded in a cry, "Quit India!" Gandhi threatens non-violent mass struggle if the cry is refused. This threat is soon taken over by undisciplined crowds and leads to the arrests of Gandhi and the Congress Working Committee. Jinnah and the British criticize the Quit India movement. A period of uneasy quiet ensues.

1943 Famine in Bengal during which millions die due to the food shortage created by war

> Appointment of Field Marshall Lord Archiebald Wavell as Viceroy

> The Provisional Government of *Azad* ("free") India declared by Bose, after which he declares war on the United States of America and Great Britain

1944 Establishment of Rangoon as Bose's capital; attempt by his army to enter India to liberate her

> C.R. Rajagopalachari's plan for a people's vote on Pakistan

> Meeting between Gandhi and Jinnah who cannot agree on the issue of separate nations

> Release of Congress leaders

1945 Surrender of Germany in May after Hitler's suicide

The War ends with the Japanese surrender in September after the Allies drop atomic bombs on Hiroshima and Nagasaki.

> Surrender of the Indian National Army; death of Bose in air crash

> Elections announced by Viceroy

> All-India Parties Conference in Simla in June to discuss the formation of an Indian government under Wavell's auspices

> Churchill replaced by Attlee

The India Burma Committee is formed by the new British Government which is sworn to granting independence.

1945–46 Elections in India in which both the Congress and the League do well

1946 Trial of the officers of the Indian National Army

Nehru espouses the officers' cause, and they are treated like heroes of the freedom struggle. This gives encouragement to the Royal Indian Navy which then mutinies at Bombay. This is the first time after the mutiny of 1858 that there is unrest in the army, and the spell of the army's loyalty to the Crown is broken.

> Insistence of Nehru and Gandhi on a United Free India; realization by Sardar Vallabhai Patel and oth-

ers that things have reached a boiling point and must
be resolved

> Prime Minister Attlee asked by Wavell for a deadline
for the end of British rule

*Prime Minister Attlee informs Parliament that a three-man
Cabinet Mission is to be sent to India to solve the crisis
there. Another conference is held at Simla at which the Mission proposes a plan of action for handing over power, which
includes setting up an interim government. However, Nehru
and Gandhi will not waver from the goal of an undivided
India, and Jinnah will not waver from his goal of dividing
India. Thus, the Mission returns to Britain. Jinnah is upset
that the Commission has returned without solving the issues
he has raised.*

> Betrayal felt by Muslims at the failure of the Mis-
sion; announcement by Jinnah of Direct Action Day

*This announcement leads to massacres in Calcutta, which
spread to other parts of the country, a tragedy that will usher
out His Majesty's Imperial Government from the subcontinent.*

> Formation of an interim government by Nehru

> Convening of the Constituent Assembly by Nehru

1947   Announcement by Attlee in the Commons that His
Majesty's Government has resolved to transfer power
to responsible Indian hands no later than June, 1948

*For reasons which are consigned to history, Britain will un-
characteristically deliver sooner, rather than later, on a
promise to India.*

> Replacement of Wavell by Admiral Lord Louis
Mountbatten

Mountbatten meets with Indian leaders while the country is torn apart by religious factions. He feels division is inevitable.

Political conditions are ready to boil over, and killings continue. Vallabhai Patel and others realize that the deadlock must be broken to prevent total chaos. V.P. Menon and Vallabhai Patel draw up a plan which appeals to both parties, partly because of the deteriorating political situation.

> Announcement by Mountbatten that India will become independent on the 15th of August, 1947; announcement of the creation of the two dominions, India and Pakistan

On midnight August 14, India is proclaimed independent and partitioned into Pakistan and India. Over ten million migrate to reach their new homes; one-tenth will lose their lives in the process.

> Pathans unleashed on Kashmir by Pakistan; war; flight of the Maharaja of Kashmir to India; accession of Kashmir to India with the stipulation that a referendum on the accession will be held at a later unspecified date

This referendum continues to be a contentious and destructive issue to this day.

> Accession of Hyderabad and Junagarh to India

> Assassination of Gandhi by Hindu fanatic who dislikes the Mahatma's secular politics

1949 Cease-fire adopted in Kashmir under the United Nations, dividing Kashmir between India and Pakistan

> Adoption of a federal constitution declaring the Republic of India

> Communist revolution in China under Mao Zhedong

> Bhoodan, or Land Gift Movement started by Acharya Vinobha Bhave, a disciple of Gandhi

Bhave accepts land for the needy on his walking tour of India.

1950 Declaration of India as a Sovereign Democratic Republic on January 26

1950–1955 First Five-Year Plan for the revival of the Indian economy

1953 Creation of Andhra Pradesh, a state of Telegu-speaking peoples

1954 Treaty of friendship between India and China

1955 Hindu Marriage Act, allowing women the right to divorce

1956 The Hindu Succession Act giving female and male heirs equal rights

> Pakistan declared an Islamic Republic

> States Re-organization Commission established to organize states on linguistic lines

> Delhi a Union Territory

> Formation of Tamil Nadu (Tamil-speaking) and Kerala (Malayali-speaking) states

1957 First Marxist Government in Kerala under E.M.S. Namboodripad

1959	*Panchayati Raj*, or the rule of village councils, based on millennia-old tradition of grassroots authority, officially declared in Rajasthan
1960	Bombay divided into the states of Gujarat and Maharashtra
1961	Tour of India by Queen Elizabeth who is treated royally
>	Goa liberated from Portugal after 450 years; resumption of Goa's position as a much-admired port of India
1962	Communist China offensive on India's borders
1963	First steps taken in planting the seeds of the Green Revolution in Indian agriculture
>	Formation of Nagaland
1964	Death of Nehru who is succeeded by his trusted friend and able comrade, Lal Bahadur Shastri
1965	India and Pakistan at war
1966	Mrs. Indira Gandhi, politician, daughter of Jawaharlal Nehru, wife of Feroze Gandhi (a freedom fighter, no relation of Mahatma Gandhi), chosen as Prime Minister
>	The Punjab divided into the states of Punjab, Haryana, and the Union Territory of Chandigarh

1968	Nobel Prize for medicine awarded to Har Gobind Singh Khorana
>	India's Green Revolution in effect
1969	Erection of statue of Gandhi in Britain by the British Government to honor his Centennial
1970	Formation of Meghalaya
1971	India on the side of the East Bengalis in their civil war, leading to war with Pakistan
>	Treaty of Peace and Friendship between India and U.S.S.R.
>	Formation of the state of Himachal Pradesh
1972	People's Republic of Bangladesh established as a Sovereign state by the former East Bengal, with Sheikh Mujibur Rahman as the Prime Minister
>	Formation of Manipur and Tripura
1973	Release by India of 90,000 Pakistani prisoners-of-war held since 1971
>	Formation of Karnataka from the old Mysore state
1974	Explosion of a nuclear device by India, the 6th nation to do so
1975	Declaration of a State of Emergency by Mrs. Gandhi, suspending all civil rights

> Death of Sarvepalli Radhakrishnan, internationally renowned scholar, President of India (1962–1967)

> Indian Federation joined by Sikkim

1977　End of Emergency called by Mrs. Gandhi

Mrs. Gandhi releases her opponents, calls for elections, and suspends ban on political parties. The Janata party wins elections, and Mrs. Gandhi's Congress Party loses.

> Resignation by Indira Gandhi after her party loses in elections; formation of new government by the Janata Party under the Prime Ministership of Morarji Desai, who plays a leading role in the freedom movement

1978　Arrest of Mrs. Gandhi on minor charges, after which she is jailed for a week

1979　Nobel Prize for Peace awarded to Mother Teresa

> Ban on cow slaughter secured by Acharya Vinobha Bhave

1980　Massive victory in national elections for Indira Gandhi's Congress I party

Mrs. Gandhi returns to Parliament in triumph.

1982　Pollution-free zone established around Taj Mahal to prevent corrosion

1983　Nobel Prize for Physics awarded to W. A. Fowler and S. Chandrasekhar for their investigation into the development of stars

>   Ethnic riots in Assam as a result of which many people become refugees

1984   "Operation Bluestar" to flush out the Sikh secessionists' occupation of the Golden Temple in Amritsar

>   Leakage of toxic gas from the Union Carbide Plant in Bhopal, which kills and injures thousands

>   Occupation of Golden Temple by the Indian Army after extremists are flushed out

>   Assassination of Mrs. Gandhi by her Sikh bodyguards

Rajiv Gandhi, son of Mrs. Gandhi, becomes the third-generation Prime Minister in his family. Riots sweep India.

1987   Formation of Arunachal Pradesh, Mizoram, and Goa as states

1989   Declaration of a *fatwa*, or edict, by the Ayatollah Khomeini of Iran, condemning Salman Rushdie, Indian-born novelist

>   Clamor by some Hindus for Ram Janma Bhoomi (the birthplace of Rama, the epic hero) at a location in legendary Ayodhya, which also houses the ancient Babri Mosque which is sacred for the Muslims

Many fatalities result from the religious violence among Hindus and Muslims.

>   Defeat of Rajiv Gandhi; V.P. Singh is the new Prime Minister

1990	Resignation of V.P. Singh afer his defeat
>	Chandrashekar elected as Prime Minister
1991	Assassination of Rajiv Gandhi by suicide bomb
1992	Narasimha Rao elected as Prime Minister
1996	H. D. Deve Gowda elected as Prime Minister
1997	50th anniversary of India's independence!

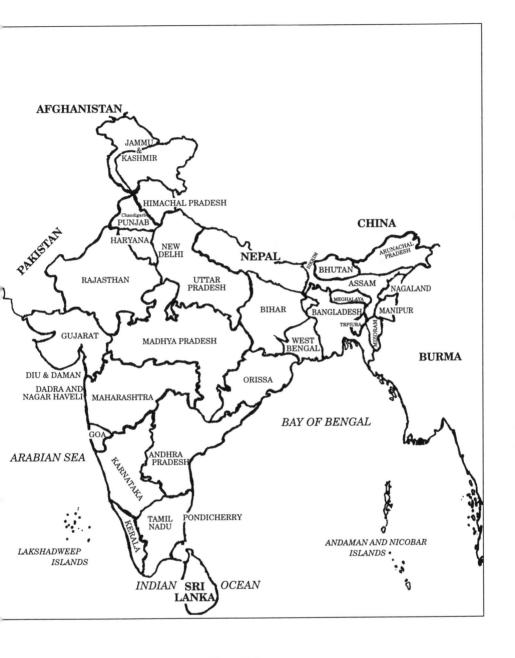

India

Select Bibliography

Akbar, M.J. (1985). *India: The Seige Within: Challenges to a Nation's Unity*. London: Penguin Books.

Akbar, M.J. (1991). *Kashmir: Behind the Vale*. Viking India.

Basham, A.L. (1994). *The Wonder that was India*. New Delhi: Rupa and Co.

Brecher, Michael. (1962). *Nehru: A Political Biography*. Boston: Beacon Press.

Coomaraswamy, A.K., and Sister Nivedita. (1967). *Myths of the Hindus and Buddhists*. New York: Dover Publications.

Durant, Will. (1954). *The Story of our Civilization: Our Oriental Heritage*. New York: Simon and Schuster.

Fischer, Louis. (1950). *The Life of Mahatma Gandhi*. New York: Harper & Row.

Fischer, Louis. (1954). *Gandhi: His Life and Message for the World*. New York: The New American Library.

Kulke, H., and Rothermund, D. (1996). *A History of India*. New York: Barnes and Noble.

Mallory, J.P. (1989). *In Search of the Indo-Europeans: Language, Archaeology and Myth*. New York: Thames and Hudson.

Nanda, B.R. (1980). *Essays in Modern Indian History*. New Delhi: Oxford University Press.

Nanda, B.R. (1996). *Mahatma Gandhi: A Biography*. New Delhi: Oxford University Press.

Nehru, Jawaharlal. (1946). *The Discovery of India*. Calcutta: The Signet Press.

Radhakrishnan, Sarvepalli and Moore, Charles. (1957). *A*

Source Book in Indian Philosophy. Princeton, New Jersey: Princeton University Press.

Spear, Percival. (1978). *Oxford History of Modern India: 1740-1975.* Oxford University Press.

Spear, Percival. (1990). *A History of India.* (Volume Two.) London: Penguin Books.

Thapar, Romila. (1979). *Ancient Indian History: Some interpretations.* New Delhi: Orient Longman.

Thapar, Romila. (1990). *A History of India.* (Volume One.) London: Penguin Books.

Wolpert, Stanley. (1993). *A New History of India.* New York and London: Oxford University Press.

Index

Brahmo Samaj 168
Britain xi, 35, 41, 44, 46, 49, 51, 55,
    57, 59, 61, 62, 65-67, 70, 72, 133,
    154, 158,163, 165-167, 171, 179,
    184, 187, 189, 190, 194, 195, 197,
    198, 200, 204
British 42, 46, 49, 82, 159
British East India Company 157,
    160, 162, 166, 167, 170, 174, 177
Buddha 10, 20, 101, 102, 108, 130, 131
Buddhism 20, 22, 23, 24, 81, 89, 101-
    104, 130, 132, 135-137, 139, 180
Bullion 40, 41
Bureaucracy 22, 126
Burke, Sir Edmund 161
Burma 25, 48, 52, 66, 169, 179, 199
Bus 3, 74, 76
Buxar 43, 159

Cabinet 71
Cabinet Mission 67, 200
Cabral, Pedro Alvarez 149
Calcutta 2, 9, 42, 43, 52, 154,
    158-160, 162, 164, 168, 170,
    173-175, 179, 187, 200
Calender 134
Calicut 39, 149
Calvin, John 151
Cambay 15, 40
Cambodia 143
Cambridge 194
Canada 70, 105, 126, 169, 187
Cannanore 149
Canning, Lord 49, 50, 174
Cape Comorin 5
Cars 76, 118
Carnatic 42, 86, 156, 157, 159, 161,
    166
Cashew Nut 150
Caste 20, 26, 27, 47, 60, 63, 95, 97-
    99, 104, 105, 129, 180
Catherine of Braganza 154
Catholic 39, 100, 150, 151
Cattle 5, 15, 18, 122
Ceylon 22, 140, 142

Chaitanya 148
Chak, Yusuf Shah 152
Chalukya 27, 28, 30, 136, 137, 140,
    141
Chanakya 22, 132
Chandrashekhar, S. 205
Chandrashekhar 205
Charaka 112, 134
Charles II 154
Charnock, Job 154
Charter Acts 167, 170, 172
Chatterjee, Bankim Chandra 53
Chauri Chaura 191
Chelmsford, Lord 59, 188, 190
Chenab River 172
Chera 24, 134, 140
Chess 85, 138
Chicken 14
Chief Election Commisioner 70
Chilies 150
China 2, 6, 13, 22, 24, 27, 41, 82, 120,
    129, 134, 135, 140, 142, 144, 153,
    171, 175, 182, 202, 203
Chinese 13, 26, 27, 41, 129, 134, 137,
    138, 171, 173
Chola 24, 28, 134, 136, 139, 140, 142
Christian 12, 24, 60, 62, 107, 108,
    136, 139, 167, 172
Christianity 33, 106, 107, 167
Christopher Columbus 149
Churchill, Sir Winston 55, 197-199
Civil Disobedience 56, 62, 189-192
Clive, Robert 42-44, 46, 157-159, 163
Cobra 8
Cochin 107, 149
Cocoon 92, 129
Coffee 83, 175
Commerce 131
Communal Award 62, 194
Communist Party of India 190
Congress Party 60, 63-65, 68, 205
Conifer 7
Connecticut 156
Constituent Assembly 65, 69, 200
Cornwallis, Lord 163, 164, 168

Cotton 16, 41, 51, 80, 165, 178, 182, 192
Council of Ministers 71, 72
Cow 18, 205
Cripps Mission 65, 66, 198
Cuisine 5, 81
Cult 136, 139, 148
Cuneiform 128
Cunningham, Sir Alexander 173
Currency 15, 32, 73, 124
Curzon, Lord 53, 181-183

Dalai Lama 153
Dalhousie, Lord 171, 172
Damodar Valley Project 7
Dance 18, 86-88, 109, 110
Danish East India Company 42, 152
Darjeeling 82, 177
Das, C.R. 60, 192
Deccan 4, 7, 24, 25, 133, 136, 139, 141, 142, 146, 151, 152, 156, 166
Deer 8
Delhi xi, 2, 26, 28-32, 38, 45, 48, 55, 73, 115, 130, 141-148, 150, 151, 155, 156, 159, 162, 183, 186, 192, 202
Devanagri 10
Dhaka xi, 165, 184
Dharma 90, 93, 95, 111
Dice 15
Doctrine of Lapse 172, 174
Dom Affonso D'Albuquerque 150
"Dot" 1, 100
Dravidian 11, 12
Dufferin, Lord 179
Dupleix, Joseph Francois 157
Durand Line 181
Durban 181
Dutch 38, 39, 42, 152, 162
Dutch East India Company 152
Dyarchy 59, 61, 189, 192
Dyer, R.E.H. Gen. 58, 190

East Pakistan xi, 69
Edward VI 183

Egypt 13, 128
Egyptian 13, 14
Election Commission 70
Electorate 54, 55, 59, 61-63, 70, 175, 186, 190, 194-196
Electricity 74
Elephant 1, 8, 110
Elgin, Lord (8th Earl) 176
Elgin, Lord (9th Earl) 181
Elizabeth, Queen 203
Elizabeth I 151
Ellora 138
Energy 7, 74, 124, 125
English 1, 9, 11, 12, 14, 38-40, 86, 90, 109, 125, 127, 144, 152-154, 162, 167, 170, 179
English East India Company 40, 42, 43, 46, 152, 154
Euphrates 13
Europe 2, 9, 22, 25, 27, 36, 38, 41, 79, 87, 107, 112, 129, 142, 143, 158, 162, 175, 193
Everest, Mt. 4

Fahein 26
Famine 50, 51, 122, 159, 178, 181, 198
Farsi 9, 10, 138, 143, 151
Farukh Siyar 155
Fatehpur Sikri 34
Fatwa 206
Federation 73, 121, 196, 205
Feline 8
Fir 7
Firdausi 29, 140
Firishta 151
Five-Year Plan 117, 118, 202
Folk Art 87
Folk Dance 87
Folk Music 88
Folk Tales 135
Folk Theatre 87
Forest 7, 8, 91, 101
Fort St. George 153
Fort William 42, 154
France 142

Tughlaq, Feroz Shah 31, 147
Tughlaq, Muhammed Ibn Tughlaq
30, 146
Tukaram 152
Tulsi Das 150
Tungabhadra River 6
Turban 1, 79
Turkey 129, 191
Tyagaraja 159

U.S.S.R. 6, 115, 126, 204
Ujjain 111, 131, 137
United States 1, 2, 6, 51, 58, 70, 72,
74, 76, 82, 96, 102, 105, 115, 119,
123, 161, 193, 198
Universal Adult Suffrage 55, 71, 185,
190
Untouchability 97
Untouchables 20, 52, 60, 62, 63, 99,
180, 194, 195
Upanishad 91, 168
Ur 129
Urban 74-77, 120, 125
Urdu 10, 11, 130, 142, 164
Urs 106
Utpala 139

Vahana 1, 91
Vaishya 20, 95
Vakataka 25, 28, 135, 136
Valmiki 92
Vampire 141
Vancouver 187
Varahamihira 112, 136
Varanasi 79, 111, 114, 130
Varuna 129
Vasco Da Gama 39, 149
Vasugupta 139
Veda Vyas 92
Veda 18, 89-91, 94, 129, 130, 139, 176
Vedic 17, 18, 89, 98, 129, 177
Vedism 89, 129
Veena 86

Vegetarian 26, 81, 104
Vernacular 10, 142
Vernacular Press Act 50
Vetalapanchavimchatika 141
Vice-President of India 71
Victoria, Queen 49, 174, 175, 178, 182
Vietnam 135
Vijayanagar 30, 142, 145-147, 150,
151
Vikramaditya 26, 141
Vindhya 5
Vishnu 96, 139, 141

Waterloo 165
Wavell, Lord 67, 68, 198, 200
Weather 6, 74, 81, 82, 114
Wedderburn, William 179
Wedding 19, 88, 143
Wellesley, Lord 161, 165, 166
Wheat 16, 81, 121, 122, 191
Wild Dogs 8
Wildlife 8
Willingdon, Lord 194
Women 18, 19, 43, 58, 78, 79, 80, 87,
109, 114, 120, 127, 158, 202
World War I 56, 57, 59, 164,189
World War II 64, 65, 67, 109

Xavier, St. Francis 151

Yadavas 30, 140
Yagnavalkya 19
Yajur Veda 90
Yale, Elihu 156
Yale University 156
Yellow River 13
Yeravada 63, 195
Yoga 93, 96, 97, 132

Zainulabidin 79, 148
Zanskar Range 4
Zoroastrian 33, 105, 107, 108, 138

About the author

Sudha Koul was born in Kashmir, India, where she com-pleted her education with a Bachelor of Arts (Honors) and a Master of Arts in Political Science. She taught Political Science at Lady Shri Ram College in New Delhi before she was selected to the Indian Administrative Service, the successor to the Indian Civil Service mentioned in this book.

Ms. Koul came to the United States after her marriage and has since raised a family in Pennington, New Jersey. She worked as the Manager of the Institute of Semitic Studies in Princeton before starting her publishing company, Cashmir, Inc.